CJ MORGAN

TRUST
ISSUES

Unbreaking What I Broke

Trust Issues

Unbreaking What I Broke

CJ Morgan

Trust Issues

Copyright © 2025 by CJ Morgan
All rights reserved.

No part of this book may be reproduced, distributed, or transmitted in any form or by any means, including photocopying, recording, or other electronic or mechanical methods, without the prior written permission of the publisher, except in the case of brief quotations embodied in critical reviews and certain other noncommercial uses permitted by copyright law. For permission requests, write to the publisher, addressed "Attention: Permissions Coordinator," at the email address below.

CJ Morgan
Houston, TX 77033
United States
yourpurpose@itzcjmorgan.com

This is a work of nonfiction. Names, characters, businesses, places, events, locales, and incidents are either the products of the author's imagination or used in a fictitious manner. Any resemblance to actual persons, living or dead, or actual events is purely coincidental.

All Scripture quotations, unless otherwise indicated, are taken from the Holy Bible, New International Version®, NIV®. Copyright ©1973, 1978, 1984, 2011 by Biblica, Inc.™ Used by permission of Zondervan. All rights reserved worldwide. www.zondervan.comThe "NIV" and "New International Version" are trademarks registered in the United States Patent and Trademark Office by Biblica, Inc.™

ISBN: 9798298754064

First Edition: August, 2025

Printed in the United States of America

Cover design by CJ Morgan
Interior design by JC Morgan
Edited by JC Morgan

For more information, visit www.itzcjmorgan.com.

Trust Issues

Dedication

To my beautiful wife, Jalika Morgan, and my incredible children, thank you for being my unwavering source of love and support. Your patience, understanding, and belief in me have carried me through the toughest moments, and your strength has helped me find mine.

To my parents, Clifton and Dinah Morgan, thank you for the foundation you've laid in my life. Your love, guidance, and sacrifices have shaped who I am today. You've always believed in me, even when I didn't believe in myself, and for that, I am forever grateful.

To my family and friends, words cannot express how grateful I am for each of you. Your encouragement, kindness, and constant prayers have lifted me when I couldn't lift myself. You've been my anchor, and I am forever thankful for the love and connection we share.

To my pastors, Jeremy and Shamika Sanders—thank you for your guidance, wisdom, and the way you've poured into my life. Your prayers and mentorship have been instrumental in my healing, and I'm grateful for the way you've always encouraged me to walk in faith, trust in God, and grow into the person I am today.

I want to keep this short, because the list is endless. If I tried to name everyone, I might miss someone. But please know this book is for you. Thank you for sticking by me through it all, pushing me to be better, praying for me, and trusting me to grow in ways I never thought possible. Your belief in me has made all the difference.

With deep appreciation,
CJ Morgan

Trust Issues

Trust Issues

Introduction

What happens when you look in the mirror and realize something you never wanted to admit?

That you have been the source of someone else's trust issues.

We spend so much time talking about what others did to us, the pain they caused, the betrayal we felt, the promises they broke. And yes, those things matter. That pain is real. But here's the uncomfortable truth: sometimes, we were the ones who did the hurting. Sometimes, we were the ones who betrayed, broke promises, walked away, or failed to show up.

And not only have we done it to others we've done it to ourselves.

Let's sit in that for a moment!

Have you ever said, "I'll never hurt you," and then did exactly that? Have you ever sworn to yourself, "I won't go back to that," and found yourself in the same situation again? Have you ever ignored someone's pain that you caused because it was easier than owning it?

Yeah. Same here.

This book was born from that space. That raw, honest place where you admit to yourself: I've caused trust issues, too.

We don't like to go there. It's much easier to point fingers. To blame everyone else. To act like we're always the victim. But real healing? Real transformation? That starts with accountability.

Trust Issues

I, CJ Morgan, wrote this book for the ones who are done pretending. For the ones who are tired of carrying the weight of what others did, but also brave enough to admit the weight of what they've done. For the ones who want to heal, who want to grow, who want to trust again but don't know how.

I've been hurt in deep ways. And I've hurt people in deep ways. I've questioned my faith, felt abandoned by God, and wondered why things didn't work out the way I prayed for. I've broken trust and had mine shattered into a million pieces. And through it all, one thing became clear: if I didn't start facing the truth, I would keep bleeding on people who didn't cut me.

So here's the truth:
- You may have trust issues because of what someone did to you.
- But someone may have trust issues because of what you did to them.
- And you might be living with the consequences of the trust you broke in yourself.

That's a lot to carry. But here's the good news: **We don't have to carry it alone.**

This book is for the bounce-back. For the rebuild. For the person staring at the rubble of their life saying, "I can't live like this anymore." Whether you've been hurt in a relationship, disappointed by a job, abandoned by friends, or felt like God didn't show up the way you needed Him to, this is for you.

Trust Issues

Because trust issues don't just make us cautious. They make us anxious. They make us controlling. They make us sabotage good things. They make us isolate. They make us bitter. They make us question everything even ourselves.

But healing is possible.

And it starts with being real. It starts with saying, "I've made mistakes, but I want to be better." It starts with getting honest about the walls we've built and the hearts we've hardened. It starts with facing ourselves, not just the people who hurt us.

This journey won't be easy, but it will be worth it. So if you're ready to be honest, if you're ready to heal, if you're ready to break the cycle... this is the book for you.

Let's go there. Let's grow through it. Let's heal together.

Track Your Progress

At the end of each chapter, you'll find pages to track your progress, reflect, or speak your heart. This isn't just about reading words it's about applying them to your life. It's about taking action. So as you work through the chapters, ask yourself the hard questions, write out your thoughts, and make sure to check in with your own growth. Healing requires effort, and I'm right here with you every step of the way.

Trust Issues

Table of Contents

The Question That Changes Everything 2

How Others Have Broken My Trust 14

Breaking the Cycle of Mistrust 22

Learning to Trust Again 34

Trusting Others Without Losing Yourself 42

Healing from Broken Trust 50

Identify Where You've Betrayed Yourself 61

The Wall 74

Trust is Trust 84

Transparency: The Heart of Trust 94

Get Back to Trusting God 104

It's Okay to Abandon the Trust Issues 114

Trust Issues

How Can I Enhance My Trust in God 124

When My Past Trust Meets the New Me 134

Trusting the Journey: Embracing Uncertainty with Faith 144

Did You Do It? Well, Own It 154

The Peace That Follows Healing 164

Stronger Relationships After Healing 174

Emotional Freedom — The Blessing of Releasing the Burden 182

The Reward of Wholeness 190

Trust Issues

Chapter One

The Question That Changes Everything

The Question That Changes Everything

There comes a moment in life when we have to stop and ask ourselves a hard question:

Do I trust myself?

Not just in a superficial way. Not just *"I trust myself to wake up and go to work"* or *"I trust myself to take care of my responsibilities."* But on a deeper level, do I trust myself to make the right decisions for my own well-being? Do I trust myself with my own heart?

Trust is something we often associate with relationships, romantic relationships, friendships, family, and even work. But what happens when the biggest betrayal we've experienced didn't come from someone else?

What happens when we realize we are the ones who let ourselves down?

The Question That Changes Everything

It's a tough pill to swallow, isn't it?

We spend so much time looking at the ways others have broken our trust. We can list every betrayal, every disappointment, every promise that was never kept. But when was the last time we took a moment to reflect on the times we betrayed ourselves?

- **The times we ignored red flags.**
- **The times we silenced our own intuition.**
- **The times we stayed in situations we knew were destroying us.**
- **The times we broke our own promises.**

Trust issues don't just come from other people. Sometimes, they come from the way we've treated ourselves.

Trust is something we talk about often, but rarely do we sit down and truly reflect on what it means. We expect it from others, we demand it in relationships, and we feel entitled to it from family and friends. But when was the last time you asked yourself: **Do I trust myself?**

Not just in a casual, surface-level way. Not just in the, "I trust myself to wake up and go to work" or "I trust myself to pay my bills" kind of way. But do I trust myself to make the right decisions? To walk away when I need to? To hold myself accountable for my own healing?

Trust Issues

See, trust isn't just about believing in others, it's about believing in ourselves.

But here's the hard truth: Many of us are walking around with broken self-trust, and we don't even realize it. We're carrying the weight of promises we made to ourselves but never kept. We're carrying the guilt of red flags we ignored. We're carrying the scars of moments where we should have listened to our intuition, but we didn't.

And yet, we wonder why trusting others feels impossible.

Now Self-trust is the foundation of every relationship we have. If we cannot trust ourselves, how can we truly trust another person? How can we expect to recognize trustworthy individuals when we don't even believe in our own ability to make sound decisions?

Many of us struggle with this silently. We make excuses for why we hesitate, why we second-guess, why we feel stuck. But at the core of it all, there's a fear: **What if I let myself down again?**

Let's take a moment to reflect. Have you ever:

- **Said you wouldn't go back to a toxic situation, only to return?**
- **Made a promise to yourself that you later broke?**
- **Ignored the little voice inside warning you of danger?**

The Question That Changes Everything

- **Stayed in a job, friendship, or relationship longer than you should have?**
- **Betrayed your own values to please someone else?**

If you answered yes to any of these, you're not alone. The truth is, we've all done this at some point. The problem isn't that we've made mistakes. The problem is that we don't address them. We don't take the time to acknowledge that **our own actions have contributed to our trust issues.**

Let's be real for a moment. Some of us are living in broken trust right now. We don't just have trust issues, we live in them. We wake up with them, we carry them into our relationships, we let them dictate our decisions. We say we want healing, but deep down, we're afraid to do the work. Why? Because healing requires accountability. It requires us to face our own role in the situation.

Here's the truth nobody wants to say out loud: **A lot of us got ourselves into the positions we're in.**

Now, that doesn't mean people didn't hurt us. It doesn't mean we deserved to be betrayed. But sometimes, we ignored the signs. We kept giving people chances when they kept showing us who they were. We stayed too long in places we should have left. And when the inevitable happened, we blamed trust itself. When in reality, we should have been questioning why we ignored our own intuition in the first place.

This isn't about shame. This isn't about beating yourself up. This is about taking your power back. Because here's the good news: **If you played a role in breaking your trust, then you can also play a role in rebuilding it.**

How Self-Trust is Formed (or Broken)

Self-trust is built over time. It's a series of choices that confirm our ability to rely on ourselves. Each time we make a decision that aligns with our values, we strengthen our self-trust. But every time we betray ourselves, we chip away at it.

Imagine self-trust as a bridge. Each time you make a decision that honors your well-being, another plank is added. But when you ignore your needs, when you go against your better judgment, a plank is removed. The more planks you remove, the shakier the bridge becomes.

Eventually, if too many planks are missing, the bridge collapses. And this is where many of us find ourselves, standing at the edge of a broken bridge, afraid to take the next step, afraid to trust again.

But here's the good news: **Bridges can be rebuilt.**

Rebuilding Trust in Yourself

Healing self-trust isn't an overnight process, but it is possible. Here's how:

The Question That Changes Everything

1. Identify Where You've Betrayed Yourself

Take a moment to reflect:

- When was the last time I ignored my intuition?
- When have I let fear stop me from making the right decision?
- Have I broken promises to myself?

Acknowledging these moments isn't about guilt, it's about awareness. You can't fix what you don't acknowledge.

2. Forgive Yourself

Instead of shame, choose grace. Instead of regret, choose growth. You are not your mistakes. You are a work in progress.

3. Start Keeping Small Promises to Yourself

Rebuilding self-trust starts with small, consistent actions. Start with manageable promises:

- "I will wake up 15 minutes earlier each morning."
- "I will drink more water today."
- "I will set a boundary and stick to it."

Each time you keep a promise to yourself, your self-trust grows stronger.

4. Listen to Your Intuition and Act on It

Your intuition is your internal guide. Start listening to it.

5. Stop Seeking External Validation

Learn to make decisions based on what feels right in your heart, not based on what other people think.

The Freedom of Self-Trust

When you trust yourself, everything changes. You:

- No longer second-guess every decision.
- Feel confident in your ability to handle challenges.
- Set boundaries without guilt.
- Recognize when a situation isn't right for you.
- Stop settling for less than you deserve.

Self-trust brings freedom. It allows you to live fully, without fear controlling your every move. It empowers you to take risks, to believe in your dreams, to trust in the process of life.

The Question That Changes Everything

So, let me ask you again: Do you trust yourself?

If the answer is no, that's okay. You are not alone in this journey. The fact that you are reading this means you are ready to change. You are ready to start rebuilding.

This is just the beginning. The work continues. But for now, take a deep breath and remember: You are worthy of your own trust.

Reflection Questions

1. When was the last time I truly put my needs first, even if it meant disappointing someone else?

2. What patterns keep showing up in my life that might be revealing where I still don't trust myself?

3. How have I silenced my intuition in the past—and what happened when I did?

4. What is one small promise I can make to myself this week—and actually keep—to start rebuilding my trust?

5. If I fully trusted myself, how would my decisions, relationships, and life be different?

The Question That Changes Everything

Chapter Two

How Others Have Broken My Trust

Trust Issues

How Others Have Broken My Trust

The Wounds of Broken Trust

Trust is fragile. It takes years to build but only moments to shatter. Most of us didn't wake up one day deciding to have trust issues. We were taught to have them through experiences that left us wounded, skeptical, and hesitant to believe in people and sometimes even ourselves.

Maybe it was a betrayal from someone we loved. Maybe it was a friend who abandoned us when we needed them the most. Maybe it was a relationship where promises were nothing more than empty words. Maybe it was someone who looked us in the eyes and swore they'd never hurt us, only to do exactly that.

Whatever it was, the result is the same: we were left questioning everything. We started doubting what people said. We second-guessed their intentions. We stopped believing that anyone could truly be trustworthy.

And that kind of pain leaves a mark. Not just on our hearts, but on the way we move through life.

Let's Be Real: The People Who Hurt Us

Let's be real, some people hurt us in ways we never thought possible. People we trusted. People we loved. People we would have done anything for.

And it's not just the big betrayals that leave scars. Sometimes it's the small things, the little disappointments that pile up over time:

- **The parent who didn't protect us when they should have.**
- **The friend who stopped showing up.**
- **The significant other who said one thing but did another.**
- **The boss who overlooked our hard work.**
- **The spiritual leader who let us down.**

Each time it happened, we told ourselves, "*I'll never let this happen again.*" And slowly, brick by brick, we built walls around our hearts, thinking they would protect us from pain.

But the truth is, those walls don't just keep the pain out, they also keep love, trust, and connection from getting in.

The Pattern of Betrayal

Here's the thing about broken trust: it often happens more than once. And after a while, we start noticing a pattern. We start to wonder:

- **Why do I keep trusting the wrong people?**
- **Why do I keep ending up in these situations?**
- **Is there something wrong with me?**

If you've ever asked yourself these questions, you're not alone. Many of us have. And while it's easy to blame others for our pain, we also have to ask ourselves an even harder question: **Why do I keep allowing it?**

That's not to say we deserved the pain. That's not to say the betrayal was our fault. But it is to say that if we don't recognize the pattern, we're doomed to repeat it.

When Broken Trust Becomes a Cycle

One of the hardest truths to face is that sometimes, broken trust isn't just about what others did to us, it's about the fact that we keep allowing certain behaviors into our lives.

- We **ignore red flags** because we want to believe the best in people.
- We **make excuses** for those who continuously let us down.
- We **give too many chances** to people who haven't earned them.
- We **settle for less than we deserve** because we're afraid to be alone.

And then, when the inevitable betrayal happens, we act surprised. But deep down, we knew. We just didn't want to admit it.

Facing this truth is painful, but it's also empowering. Because once we see the pattern, we can break it.

How Broken Trust Changes Us

When someone breaks our trust, it doesn't just hurt, it changes us.

We become:

- **Guarded and distant.**
- **Quick to assume the worst.**
- **Afraid of vulnerability.**
- **Slow to open up to new people.**
- **Skeptical of kindness and good intentions.**

And the saddest part? We don't even realize we've changed. We think we're just being "*careful*" or "*wise*," but in reality, we're living in fear. We're letting past betrayals dictate our future relationships.

We think we're protecting ourselves, but really, we're imprisoning ourselves in isolation.

Let's Be Honest: The Hardest Part of Healing

The hardest part of healing from broken trust isn't forgiving others, it's learning to trust again. It's allowing ourselves to be open, knowing we might get hurt again.

Because the truth is, no matter how much we try to protect ourselves, we can't live a full life without trust. We can't have deep relationships. We can't experience true love. We can't build meaningful connections.

So, we have a choice:

- **Stay guarded and live in fear.**
- **Take the risk and learn to trust again.**

It won't happen overnight. It won't be easy. But the first step is recognizing that trust is a choice we have to make, despite the pain we've endured.

Acknowledging the Pain, Choosing to Heal

Healing starts with awareness. And as painful as it is to relive betrayal, it's necessary if we ever want to move forward.

This chapter isn't about staying stuck in the pain. It's about acknowledging it so we can heal. Trust issues don't just disappear, we have to actively work through them. And the first step is recognizing the wounds left behind by others and ourselves. We must decide that they won't control us anymore.

Broken trust may have shaped you, but it doesn't have to define you. You get to decide what comes next.

Reflection Questions

1. Who are the people that have broken your trust the most?

2. How have those experiences shaped the way you see people today?

3. Are you carrying trust issues into relationships that don't deserve them?

4. Have you built walls so high that no one can get close to you?

Trust Issues

Chapter Three

Breaking the Cycle of Mistrust

Breaking the Cycle of Mistrust

By now, we've acknowledged the reality of broken trust both in ourselves and in others. We've faced the painful truth that trust is not just something others violate, but something we often struggle to uphold within ourselves. We've explored the emotional toll that comes with living in a state of distrust. But now, we come to the most important question: **How do we break the cycle?**

Because let's be real, many of us are stuck in a pattern of mistrust. We expect betrayal before it happens. We hesitate to get close to people. We assume the worst because, in the past, the worst is what we got. But living this way is exhausting. It's lonely. It's limiting. And it keeps us from the deep, meaningful connections we crave.

So, how do we break free? How do we finally step out of this cycle and start rebuilding trust, not just in others, but in ourselves?

Recognizing the Patterns

Before we can change anything, we have to first recognize the habits that keep us trapped in mistrust. It's easy to ignore or minimize these behaviors because they feel protective, they're the way we've learned to cope. But in reality, these habits don't protect us; they isolate us and keep us stuck in a cycle of fear and loneliness.

Have you ever found yourself:

- **Pushing people away before they have the chance to hurt you?**
- **Assuming everyone has an ulterior motive?**
- **Overanalyzing people's words and actions, looking for hidden betrayals?**
- **Feeling the need to constantly "test" others to see if they are trustworthy?**
- **Avoiding vulnerability because it feels too risky?**

If you've answered yes to any of these, you're not alone. These behaviors are survival tactics. They're our way of protecting ourselves. But in reality, they don't protect us. They keep us from real connection, from building relationships that are healthy, fulfilling, and rooted in trust.

The first step in breaking the cycle of mistrust is to recognize when we are stuck in it. Only when we acknowledge the problem can we begin to make the changes that will lead to healing and freedom.

Let's Be Real: Fear is Controlling Us

At the root of most of our mistrust is fear. Fear of being hurt again. Fear of looking foolish. Fear of making the wrong choice. Fear of opening up, only to be let down once more. It's a fear that, if left unchecked, controls us and dictates how we interact with others.

Fear convinces us that staying closed off is the safer option. It whispers, "Don't trust them, they'll hurt you, just like the last person did." And so, we stay guarded. We stay distant. We don't let anyone in. We might even push people away before they have the chance to hurt us. And yet, in doing so, we miss out on the very thing we want most: **connection.**

But here's the uncomfortable truth we need to face: **If we let fear control us, we will never heal.** We will never experience deep love, real friendships, or authentic relationships if we don't learn to take the risk of trusting again.

Let's be clear, trust isn't just about others. It's also about ourselves. If we can't trust ourselves to make the right decisions, how can we trust others to do the same? If we don't have the courage to be vulnerable, how can we expect others to open up to us?

Healing Starts with a Choice

Trust isn't something that just magically appears one day. It's a choice. A decision we have to make, even when it feels impossible. It's about deciding to give people the chance to earn trust again, despite the wounds of the past. And it's about choosing to let go of the fear that keeps us stuck.

Here's how we start breaking the cycle:

1. Identify Where Mistrust is Holding You Back

The first step is awareness. Without recognizing where mistrust is affecting our lives, we can't begin to address it. So, ask yourself:

- **Where in my life is mistrust keeping me from happiness?**
- **Am I pushing people away who haven't actually done anything wrong?**
- **Have I let past experiences define my present and future?**

Awareness is key. You can't change something you're not willing to face. If you don't acknowledge where mistrust is affecting your relationships, your career, or your self-worth, you can't begin the healing process.

2. Stop Punishing New People for Old Wounds

One of the most damaging things we do is carry our past betrayals into new relationships. Just because someone else hurt you doesn't mean the next person will. Yes, be cautious. Yes, use wisdom. But don't assume that everyone is out to hurt you. Don't make the new person pay for the mistakes of someone else.

You're allowed to be cautious. You're allowed to take time to trust. But you also need to give people the opportunity to show you their true character. Let them prove themselves, and don't assume the worst before they've even had the chance to show you who they really are.

3. Set Healthy Boundaries (Not Walls)

There's a difference between having healthy boundaries and completely shutting people out. Many of us have become so afraid of being hurt that we've built walls, massive, impenetrable walls. But walls are not the answer.

- **Walls** say, "No one gets in. Ever."

- **Boundaries** say, "I will allow people in, but only in a way that respects my needs and well-being."

Boundaries are protective; walls are imprisoning. You can't heal in isolation. You need relationships. You need connection. But you also need to protect your peace. Learning the difference between boundaries and walls is crucial to breaking the cycle of mistrust.

4. Learn to Trust Yourself Again

A huge part of breaking the cycle is rebuilding self-trust. If you don't trust yourself to make good decisions, you'll never feel safe trusting others. If you don't trust your own judgment, you'll be constantly second-guessing everyone around you.

Start small:

- Make a commitment to yourself and keep it.
- Listen to your intuition when something feels off.
- Acknowledge your past mistakes but remind yourself that you've grown.

The more you trust yourself, the easier it becomes to trust others. And the more you honor your own boundaries, the easier it will be to trust that others will honor them too.

5. Take the Risk—But With Wisdom

Trust is always a risk. It's scary to open up to people after you've been hurt. But it's also necessary. Trust is the foundation of every meaningful relationship, and without it, we live in isolation.

Taking the risk doesn't mean blindly trusting everyone who comes your way. It means using discernment. It means giving people the opportunity to prove their character over time. It means understanding that trust isn't about perfection, it's about consistency. It's about seeing people for who they are and allowing them to show up in your life as they truly are, not as the person you fear they might become.

Moving Forward: Choosing a Different Future

Breaking the cycle of mistrust isn't easy. It requires intentional effort. It requires courage. But most of all, it requires a willingness to change.

The past may have shaped us, but it doesn't have to define us. We have the power to rewrite our stories. We can choose to trust again. We can choose healing. We can choose freedom.

The cycle doesn't have to keep repeating itself. Each day is a new opportunity to make a different choice. Each moment is a chance to break free from the patterns that have kept us trapped.

So, what will you choose?

The cycle of mistrust is not a life sentence. It's a challenge to overcome, but it's also a chance for transformation. As you continue this journey, remember: You have the power to break free. You have the ability to heal. You can rebuild trust, both in others and in yourself. It starts with the decision to choose differently, to embrace vulnerability, and to walk in the freedom that only comes from living with an open heart.

Trust Issues

Let this be the chapter where you choose to break the cycle for good.

Reflection Questions

1. In what ways has mistrust shaped your relationships?

2. Are you willing to take small steps toward trusting again?

3. What boundaries do you need to set to protect yourself while still allowing connection?

4. How can you start rebuilding trust in yourself?

Trust Issues

Breaking the Cycle of Mistrust

Chapter Four

Learning to Trust Again

Learning to Trust Again

The Fear of Trusting Again

By now, we've unpacked the weight of mistrust. We've faced the painful reality that trust isn't just something others break, but something we also struggle to maintain within ourselves. Now comes the real challenge: **learning to trust again.**

Let's be real, this is where most of us get stuck. We acknowledge our trust issues. We recognize how they hold us back. But when it comes to actually taking that step forward? Fear grips us. Doubt paralyzes us. And suddenly, trusting again feels impossible.

But is it? Or is it just that we've become so accustomed to our walls that we don't know how to live without them?

The Scars That Keep Us Guarded

Every betrayal, every letdown, every broken promise has left a scar. Some of these scars are so deep that we stop believing trust is even an option. Instead, we tell ourselves things like:

- *"I can't afford to be hurt again."*
- *"People always disappoint me."*

- *"If I don't expect anything, I won't be let down."*
- *"I'm better off keeping my distance."*

We convince ourselves that our mistrust is a shield. A way to stay safe. But in reality, it's a prison. It keeps us from experiencing the very things we crave such as love, connection, belonging, and peace.

The truth is, refusing to trust doesn't prevent pain; it only guarantees loneliness.

Let's Be Real: Trust Will Always Be a Risk

We want guarantees. We want to know that if we open our hearts again, we won't be let down. We want assurances that if we trust, we won't regret it.

But life doesn't work that way.

The hard truth? Trust will always be a risk. There is no way to avoid it. Even the strongest, healthiest relationships come with the possibility of disappointment. But the alternative, living in constant suspicion and isolation, is even worse.

So, the real question isn't *"Can I trust again?"* The question is: *"Am I willing to risk trusting again, knowing that it might not be perfect?"*

The Steps to Rebuilding Trust

If you've been living with trust issues for a long time, you won't heal overnight. It's a process. But like any process, it begins with small, intentional steps.

Trust Issues

1. Acknowledge That Trust Issues Are Holding You Back

You cannot change what you refuse to confront. Take a hard look at your life and ask yourself:

- How many opportunities have I missed because of mistrust?
- How many relationships have suffered because I couldn't let go of past hurts?
- How has my inability to trust affected my happiness, my peace, my future?

Awareness is the first step to healing. You have to recognize the weight of your mistrust before you can begin to release it.

2. Differentiate Between Caution and Fear

Not trusting blindly is wise. But refusing to trust at all is fear. There's a difference between being cautious and being emotionally unavailable.
Caution says: *"I will take my time getting to know someone's character before I trust them."*
Fear says: *"I refuse to let anyone in because I might get hurt."*
Caution says: *"I will set boundaries to protect myself."*
Fear says: *"I will build walls so high that no one can ever reach me."*
Are you being cautious? Or are you living in fear?

3. Learn to Trust Yourself First

Most trust issues don't actually start with other people. They start with us.
If you don't trust yourself to make good decisions, to recognize red flags, or to walk away when necessary, you will

Learning to Trust Again

struggle to trust others. Healing begins with rebuilding self-trust.

How do you do this?

- Start keeping the promises you make to yourself.
- Set standards and stick to them.
- Stop ignoring your intuition.
- Forgive yourself for past mistakes and recognize your growth.

The stronger your self-trust, the easier it becomes to extend trust to others.

4. Trust in Stages, Not All at Once

One mistake we make is thinking that trust is all or nothing. It's not. You don't have to hand someone your heart, your secrets, or your faith in one instant. Trust is built in stages.

Think of trust like a ladder. One step at a time. One small act of consistency at a time. One moment of honesty at a time.

Let people show you who they are over time. Don't force trust. Allow it to grow naturally.

5. Accept That Trust Will Be Tested

Even the healthiest relationships will have moments where trust is challenged. No one is perfect. People will make mistakes. Disappointments will happen.

But here's what matters: **how you handle it.**

When trust is tested, you have two choices:

- **React out of fear** and assume the worst.

- **Respond with wisdom** and seek understanding.

Not every mistake is a betrayal. Not every disagreement is a reason to shut down. Learn the difference between an honest mistake and intentional deception.

6. Give Yourself Permission to Try Again

If you've been hurt, it's understandable to feel hesitant. It's okay to take your time. But don't let your past dictate your future.
You deserve love. You deserve healthy relationships. You deserve peace.

And you won't get those things if you refuse to trust.

Moving Forward: Choosing Trust Over Fear

You have a choice. You can continue living in the cycle of mistrust, always waiting for the next letdown, always keeping people at a distance. Or, you can take a step forward.
It won't be easy. It won't be comfortable. But healing never is.
Trusting again doesn't mean being naïve. It doesn't mean pretending the hurt never happened. It means choosing to move forward despite the hurt.
Because the truth is, **trusting again isn't about the other person. It's about you.**

It's about freeing yourself from the chains of fear. It's about opening your heart to the possibility of love, joy, and connection. It's about no longer letting past wounds dictate your future.
So, take the step. Start small. But start.

Because you are worth it.

Reflection Questions

1. What is one area of your life where mistrust is holding you back?

2. What is one small step you can take toward trusting again?

3. How can you rebuild trust in yourself before extending it to others?

4. Are you willing to let go of fear and take the risk of trust again?

Trust Issues

Chapter Five

Trusting Others Without Losing Yourself

Trusting Others Without Losing Yourself

The Fear of Opening Up

Let's be honest trusting others after being hurt is terrifying. The idea of opening up, of being vulnerable again, feels like walking into the same fire that once burned us. It's natural to hesitate. It's understandable to question whether it's even worth the risk.

But here's a truth we need to confront: **Mistrust doesn't protect us. It isolates us.**

We tell ourselves that keeping our guard up keeps us safe. But in reality, it just keeps us alone. We crave deep connections, love, and relationships, but we keep people at arm's length out of fear.

So how do we break this cycle? How do we begin to trust others again without losing ourselves in the process?

Recognizing the Signs of Self-Betrayal

Before we can trust others in a healthy way, we have to address the ways we've abandoned ourselves in the past. Too often, mistrust isn't just about what others have done to us it's about the times we ignored our own instincts, silenced our own voices, and dismissed the truth we already knew deep down.

Ask yourself:

- Have I ignored my gut feelings in past relationships?
- Have I stayed in situations that were clearly unhealthy?
- Have I lowered my standards just to keep someone around?
- Have I trusted people who consistently showed me they couldn't be trusted?

These moments of self-betrayal hurt just as much as external betrayals. Maybe even more. Because when we can't trust ourselves, trusting others feels impossible.

Let's Be Real: Not Everyone Deserves Your Trust

Here's where we need to get honest: **Not everyone is trustworthy.** And that's okay.

Trusting others doesn't mean blindly handing our hearts to anyone who asks for it. It means using wisdom. It means recognizing the difference between someone who has **earned** our trust and someone who is simply demanding it.

So let's make one thing clear: **Healthy trust is built, it's not given freely.**

How Do You Know Who Deserves Your Trust?

Pay attention to the following:

- **Consistency:** Do their actions align with their words?
- **Integrity:** Do they do the right thing even when no one is watching?

- **Respect for Boundaries:** Do they honor your needs and limits, or do they push them?
- **Accountability:** Do they take responsibility when they mess up, or do they shift blame?
- **Emotional Safety:** Do you feel safe expressing yourself, or do you feel judged and dismissed?

People show us who they are over time. Trust isn't built in a single moment, it's built through consistent, reliable behavior.

Setting Boundaries Without Building Walls

When we've been hurt, we tend to overcorrect. Instead of setting boundaries, we build walls. We shut people out entirely, assuming that no trust is safer than risking broken trust.

But here's the problem: **Walls keep out the bad, but they also keep out the good.**

Boundaries, on the other hand, allow us to engage with others in a way that protects our peace without isolating ourselves.

Healthy Boundaries Look Like:

- Saying no without guilt
- Walking away from toxic situations without second-guessing yourself
- Taking your time to trust someone instead of rushing into deep connections
- Prioritizing your needs and well-being, even in relationships
- Allowing yourself space to process emotions before reacting

Boundaries are a sign of self-respect, not mistrust. They allow us to navigate relationships in a way that honors our healing while still remaining open to connection.

The Difference Between Trust and Dependency

Trusting others doesn't mean losing yourself in them. Too often, we mistake trust for dependence, we give too much, sacrifice too much, and end up feeling empty when the relationship doesn't work out.

So let's be clear: Trust is about security, not survival.

You can trust someone and still:

- Maintain your own identity
- Have your own opinions, beliefs, and boundaries
- Say no when something doesn't feel right
- Walk away if the relationship is no longer healthy

Trust should never require you to shrink yourself. If it does, it's not trust, it's control.

Rebuilding Trust: One Step at a Time

If you've been living in the shadows of mistrust for a long time, this process won't happen overnight. And that's okay. Healing is not a race. It's a journey.

Steps to Start Trusting Again:

1. Trust Yourself First. If you don't trust yourself, you won't trust anyone else. Start by listening to your intuition and honoring your own needs.
2. Let People Prove Themselves. Don't force trust, let it grow naturally through consistent actions.
3. Set Boundaries Early. Make it clear what is and isn't acceptable to you in relationships.
4. Don't Ignore Red Flags. If something feels off, pay attention. Trust is built on discernment, not blind faith.
5. Accept That Trust Involves Risk. There's no way around it, trusting again means risking disappointment. But the alternative, living in fear and isolation, is even worse.

Moving Forward: Choosing Trust with Wisdom

At the end of the day, trusting others isn't about being naive. It's not about pretending you haven't been hurt. It's about refusing to let that hurt define you.

Yes, you've been let down. Yes, people have broken your trust before. But that doesn't mean everyone will. And it doesn't mean you have to live your life behind walls of fear.

Trust again, but do it wisely. Give trust where it's earned. Protect your peace. Honor your boundaries. And most of all, trust yourself enough to know that no matter what happens, you'll be okay.

Because you are stronger than your past. And your future is waiting.

Reflection Question

1. Am I keeping people out to protect myself—or because I don't trust myself to choose wisely?

2. Have I confused setting boundaries with building walls—and what has that cost me in my relationships?

3. Who in my life has shown me they're consistent, respectful, and emotionally safe—but I still struggle to trust them? Why?

4. What are my non-negotiables when it comes to trust—and have I been honoring them, or compromising them?

5. How can I practice trusting others without abandoning myself in the process?

Chapter Six

Healing from Broken Trust

Healing from Broken Trust

The Weight of Broken Trust

Broken trust is heavy. It lingers in our minds, sits in our hearts, and follows us into every new relationship, every new opportunity, every new chance at connection. It shapes how we see the world and, more importantly, how we see ourselves.

When someone we trusted betrays us, it does more than just hurt, it shifts our entire sense of safety. We question everything: **Was I blind? Was I naive? How did I let this happen?** And perhaps the most painful question of all: **Will I ever be able to trust again**?

We carry the weight of those betrayals like baggage, dragging them from one situation to the next, never fully unpacking them, never fully healing from them. Instead of addressing the wound, we just cover it, hoping time alone will make it go away.

But let's be real: **Time doesn't heal wounds, intentional healing does.**

The Emotional Aftermath of Betrayal

Being betrayed isn't just about the act itself, it's about the ripple effects that follow. Betrayal shakes our foundation. It can leave us feeling:

- **Angry** – Not just at the person who hurt us, but at ourselves for trusting them.
- **Ashamed** – Wondering if we should have seen the signs, if we should have known better.
- **Unworthy** – Questioning whether we were ever truly valued or respected.
- **Fearful** – Afraid to open up again, afraid to be vulnerable, afraid to trust.
- **Numb** – Shutting down emotionally because feeling nothing feels safer than feeling everything.

These emotions don't just go away on their own. They don't fade because we ignore them. If anything, they grow stronger the longer they go unaddressed.

So, how do we move forward? How do we heal from broken trust when every part of us feels stuck in the pain?

Step One: Acknowledge the Hurt

We can't heal what we refuse to face. Many of us try to bypass the pain, pretending we're "fine" when we're not. We tell ourselves to "move on" before we've even processed what happened. But suppressing emotions only leads to them resurfacing in unhealthy ways later.

Acknowledge what happened. Say it out loud. Write it down. Let yourself feel the weight of it without judgment.

Ask yourself:

- How did this betrayal make me feel?
- What fears or doubts did it create in me?
- What beliefs about myself or others did it change?

Facing the pain is uncomfortable, but it's the first step toward releasing it.

Step Two: Separate the Action from Your Identity

When we're betrayed, we often internalize it. We start believing that we were the problem. That we were too trusting, too foolish, too weak. But trust isn't a flaw, and being hurt doesn't mean we deserved it.

Say this to yourself: **What they did is a reflection of them, not me.**

You were not betrayed because you were "too much" or "not enough." You were betrayed because someone else chose to act in a way that was dishonest, hurtful, or selfish. Their actions do not define your worth.

Step Three: Stop Replaying the Story

Our minds love to revisit painful moments, searching for clues, replaying conversations, analyzing every detail to figure out where things went wrong. But reliving the betrayal over and over doesn't change what happened, it just keeps us trapped in the pain.

Healing requires us to stop living in the past and start focusing on the present. When you catch yourself replaying the betrayal, gently redirect your mind:

- Instead of asking, "Why did this happen to me?" ask, "What can I learn from this?"
- Instead of dwelling on what was lost, focus on what can be gained: wisdom, strength, resilience.
- Instead of letting pain define you, let growth shape you.

Step Four: Learn to Trust Yourself Again

The hardest part of healing isn't learning to trust others it's learning to trust ourselves.

After betrayal, we doubt our own judgment. We wonder if we can recognize red flags, if we can trust our intuition, if we'll ever feel safe again.

Rebuilding self-trust means:

- **Honoring your gut feelings** instead of ignoring them.
- **Setting boundaries** and sticking to them.
- **Being kind to yourself** instead of blaming yourself.
- **Following through on your promises to yourself**—no more making excuses for people who don't deserve a second chance.

The more you trust yourself, the less power betrayal will have over you.

Step Five: Choose Forgiveness—But on Your Terms

Forgiveness isn't about excusing the betrayal. It's not about saying it was okay or pretending it didn't hurt. Forgiveness is about freeing yourself from the weight of resentment.

Holding on to anger doesn't protect you, it only poisons you. It keeps the wound fresh instead of allowing it to heal. But forgiveness isn't something you do for them, it's something you do for yourself.

That being said, forgiveness doesn't mean reconciliation. You can forgive someone without letting them back into your life. You can release the pain without reopening the door.

Forgiveness is a choice. And when you're ready, it's one of the most powerful choices you can make.

Step Six: Open Your Heart Again—When You're Ready

Healing from broken trust doesn't mean you have to rush into trusting again. It's okay to take your time. It's okay to go slow. But don't let one betrayal rob you of future joy.

Not everyone is untrustworthy. Not everyone will hurt you. There are people who will honor your trust, respect your boundaries, and love you the way you deserve.

The key is to move forward with wisdom, not fear. To trust again not blindly, but intentionally.

You Are Not Your Pain

Betrayal may have changed you, but it doesn't have to define you. You are not the pain you've experienced. You are not the brokenness you've felt.

Healing from Broken Trust

You are someone who is healing. Someone who is learning. Someone who is reclaiming their power, one step at a time.

And trust? It may take time, but it is possible. Not because others are perfect, but because you are strong enough to navigate trust with wisdom, grace, and courage.

Your heart is still capable of love. Your soul is still capable of connection. And your future is still wide open, waiting for you to step into it free from the chains of broken trust.

Because you deserve that. You always have.

Reflection Questions

1. Am I still carrying pain from a betrayal I've never fully faced?

2. Have I made someone else's betrayal a statement about my worth?

3. What story about trust or love have I been replaying—and is it time to rewrite that story?

4. Do I truly trust myself right now?

5. Am I holding on to resentment that's holding me back?

Trust Issues

Chapter Seven

Identify Where You've Betrayed Yourself

Trust Issues

Chapter Seven

Identify Where You've Betrayed Yourself

Let's talk about something most people avoid: self-betrayal. It's not comfortable. It's not easy to admit. But it's necessary if we're ever going to truly heal from the trust issues that have kept us guarded, isolated, and afraid to hope.

You can't talk about trust without talking about self-trust. And you can't talk about self-trust without looking honestly at the moments where you betrayed yourself. Because here's the truth…some of the deepest wounds we carry weren't inflicted by others. They were the result of our own choices, compromises, and silence.

Let's be real: it's hard to admit you hurt yourself. It's hard to face the fact that some of the pain you're dealing with today is a direct result of decisions you made when you knew better but didn't do better. But this isn't about guilt or shame…it's about truth. Because truth is the beginning of freedom.

The Silent Killer: Self-Betrayal

Self-betrayal doesn't always scream. Sometimes it whispers. It's subtle. It shows up in moments when you ignore your intuition. When you silence your voice to keep the peace. When you abandon your values for the sake of being accepted. When you keep giving chances to someone who keeps proving they don't deserve them.

It looks like:

- Staying in toxic relationships because you're afraid of being alone.
- Saying yes when your soul is screaming no.
- Downplaying your worth to make someone else comfortable.
- Breaking promises to yourself over and over again.

Every time you do this, a little piece of you gets chipped away. And over time, those pieces become harder and harder to recover.

Why We Betray Ourselves

Nobody wakes up one day and decides, "I'm going to betray myself today." It usually comes from survival. From fear. From old wounds and learned behaviors.

Identify Where You've Betrayed Yourself

We betray ourselves because:

- We don't want to be rejected.
- We think we don't deserve better.
- We were taught to prioritize others over ourselves.
- We're addicted to potential instead of reality.
- We mistake suffering for love.

But just because it's understandable doesn't mean it's acceptable. Because every time we betray ourselves, we reinforce the belief that we aren't worthy of protection...even from ourselves.

The Cost of Self-Betrayal

Let's be clear: self-betrayal is expensive. It costs you your peace. Your confidence. Your clarity. It makes it hard to hear your own voice. It makes you question your judgment. It keeps you in cycles that are toxic, repetitive, and exhausting.

And the worst part? It leads to resentment. You start resenting others for taking advantage of you, but deep down, you're really angry at yourself...for letting it happen. For not walking away. For not speaking up. For knowing better and doing it anyway.

That kind of internal conflict is heavy. It doesn't go away on its own. It festers. It shows up in how you talk to yourself, how you treat your body, how you move through the world. And the only way to heal it is to face it.

Let's Be Really Honest… With Ourselves

This isn't about blame. This is about ownership. Owning the fact that some of the trust issues we're navigating didn't just come from others…they came from us.

So, let's be honest:

- Have you ignored your gut to avoid conflict?
- Have you downplayed your feelings so you wouldn't seem "too much"?
- Have you let someone come back into your life who didn't deserve access?
- Have you broken your own boundaries just to keep the peace?

If the answer is yes, you're not alone. We've all done it. But the power is in recognizing it and deciding to do something different moving forward.

The Mirror Doesn't Lie

Looking in the mirror and admitting that you've been the one causing harm to yourself? That's not easy. But it's one of the bravest things you'll ever do. Because in that moment, you stop being a victim of your circumstances and you become an architect of your healing.

The mirror doesn't lie. And when you finally look at yourself and say, "I'm done hurting me," you begin to take back your power.

How to Rebuild Trust with Yourself

1. Acknowledge the betrayal – Write it down. Speak it out loud. Say the hard things. "I betrayed myself when I stayed with someone who didn't value me." "I betrayed myself when I chose their comfort over my peace." Honesty is the first step.

2. Grieve what you lost – You lost time. You lost energy. You lost versions of yourself that believed in more. Don't skip this step. Grieve it. Cry for it. Mourn the opportunities and joy you sacrificed.

3. Make new commitments – Self-trust is built just like any other trust…through consistency. Start with small promises. "I will speak up when something doesn't feel right." "I will rest when I'm tired." "I will say no without guilt."

4. Hold yourself accountable – When you mess up (and you will), don't beat yourself up. Hold yourself accountable! Learn from it. Grow from it. But don't abandon yourself all over again.

5. Speak to yourself with compassion – You didn't betray yourself because you're weak. You did it because you were scared. Because you didn't know better. Because you were surviving. Be kind to yourself as you heal.

6. Protect your peace – You don't owe access to people who make you betray yourself. Set boundaries. Walk away. Cut ties. You don't have to justify protecting your peace.

Reparenting the Parts That Were Taught to Betray Themselves

A lot of our self-betrayal comes from childhood. Maybe you grew up in a home where your voice didn't matter. Maybe you were taught that love meant sacrifice…even if it cost you your happiness. Maybe you were praised for being quiet, obedient, agreeable.

And now, as an adult, you're still performing for acceptance.

Reparenting means going back to that little version of you and saying, "I'm sorry. I see you. I'm not going to silence you anymore." It means teaching yourself a new way to exist. One where your needs matter. Your voice matters. Your peace matters.

The Relationship Between Self-Betrayal and Trust Issues

It's impossible to have healthy relationships with others if your relationship with yourself is built on betrayal. Because here's what happens:

Identify Where You've Betrayed Yourself

- You'll attract people who mirror your lack of self-respect.
- You'll tolerate behavior that matches your internal self-worth.
- You'll confuse chaos with passion.
- You'll stay in places that feel familiar, even if they're unhealthy.

Healing trust issues starts inside. When you trust yourself, you naturally demand that others treat you with the same respect. When you honor your boundaries, you stop tolerating people who don't. When you value your voice, you stop shrinking for love.

What Self-Trust Looks Like in Real Life

- Saying no without explaining yourself.
- Walking away from disrespect the first time.
- Listening to your gut even when it's inconvenient.
- Taking time to process instead of people-pleasing.
- Showing up for yourself the way you wish others would.

Self-trust isn't about being perfect. It's about being present with yourself. It's about choosing you even when it's hard. It's about believing that you're worth protecting, even from your own bad habits.

Forgive Yourself

This is the part most people skip...but it's crucial.

Forgive yourself for:

- The times you didn't know better.
- The times you did know better but still stayed.
- The ways you dimmed your light.
- The peace you traded for approval.

Forgiveness doesn't mean what you did was okay. It means you're no longer going to hold yourself hostage to the past. It means you've decided to stop punishing yourself and start loving yourself back to life.

Let's Be Really Real for a Moment

You can't keep blaming your ex, your parents, your boss, your friends. If you keep betraying yourself, nothing else will change.

It doesn't matter how much therapy you go to. It doesn't matter how many devotionals you read. It doesn't matter how many boundaries you try to set.

If you keep betraying yourself, you'll keep resetting the cycle.

The change starts when you say, "No more." When you decide that you're not going to be your own enemy anymore.

Identify Where You've Betrayed Yourself

When you choose truth over comfort. When you stop abandoning yourself every time love, approval, or fear comes knocking.

That's the moment everything shifts.

You Deserve to Be Safe with You

At the end of the day, the one person you spend your entire life with…is you. And if you don't feel safe within yourself, no relationship, no career, no spiritual practice will feel secure either.

So start here. Start with truth. Start with ownership. Start with grace.

Rebuild the trust you lost with yourself. Make yourself a safe place again.

Because when you do, everything else starts to shift. Your standards change. Your relationships improve. Your confidence rises. Your peace becomes non-negotiable.

You were never meant to live in a cycle of self-betrayal. You were meant to live in wholeness. And it's not too late to return to yourself.

Reflection Questions

1. When was the last time you betrayed yourself, and why?

2. What patterns of self-betrayal do you see repeating in your life?

3. What would it look like to start protecting yourself instead of abandoning yourself?

4. Who are you when you're not trying to be accepted?

5. What promises can you start keeping to rebuild your self-trust?

6. How can you speak more kindly and truthfully to yourself moving forward?

Identify Where You've Betrayed Yourself

Trust Issues

Chapter Eight

The Wall

The Wall

Let's be real. Most of us have built walls. Brick by brick, moment by moment, betrayal by betrayal…we've built them. And they didn't show up overnight. They were formed slowly, shaped by pain, disappointment, and the fear that if we don't protect ourselves, we'll be destroyed by the next person who comes too close.

But here's the question: Are those walls really protecting you…or are they just keeping you isolated from the love, connection, and healing you actually crave?

Walls feel safe. That's why we build them. They feel like protection. But over time, the same wall we built to keep hurt out, also keeps healing out. And in the name of survival, we end up slowly dying inside.

Where the Wall Began

Maybe you don't even remember when you started building it. Maybe it was your first heartbreak. Maybe it was your father not showing up. Maybe it was that friend who told your secret, the one you trusted. Or maybe it was the slow erosion of trust in a relationship that promised forever but gave you pain instead.

The Wall

Whatever it was, it planted a seed. A belief that said, "You can't let people in. It's not safe." And from that moment on, the wall started going up.

Some walls are made of sarcasm. Some of silence. Some of pretending everything is okay when you're really falling apart. Some of anger. Some of detachment. But they all serve the same purpose, to protect a wounded heart.

The False Security of Emotional Walls

The truth is, emotional walls give the illusion of safety. You think, "If I never open up, no one can hurt me." And on the surface, that's true. But underneath? You're still hurting. You're just hurting alone.

You still feel the ache of unmet connection. You still long for intimacy. You still want someone to see you and stay. But the wall makes it impossible. Because in order to love and be loved, to know and be known, you have to be seen. And the wall blocks all of that.

Let's be real: You might be surviving behind your wall, but are you living?

What the Wall Costs You

Walls don't just block out pain. They block out:

- Love
- Opportunities
- Intimacy
- Growth
- Healing
- Community

Trust Issues

They block out your future.

You can't fully show up to your purpose when you're hiding behind fear. You can't love freely when your hands are too busy guarding your heart. You can't experience the fullness of joy if you're constantly preparing for pain.

And most of all, you can't trust again if you never take the wall down.

Let's Be Really Honest...

You say you want a real relationship, but you don't let people close. You say you want healing, but you won't let anyone touch your wounds. You say you want connection, but you're still checking for exits every time someone shows up.

Here's the hard truth: the wall might have been necessary once. Maybe it did protect you back then. But now? It's holding you hostage.

Why We Keep the Wall Up

We keep the wall up because we're scared.

- Scared to be hurt again.
- Scared to be disappointed.
- Scared to look foolish.
- Scared that what happened last time will happen again.

Fear is a powerful architect. It builds high. It builds strong. And if you're not careful, fear will make you believe that isolation is strength.

But let's get this straight: avoiding vulnerability isn't strength…it's survival. And survival isn't living.

The Wall Feels Like Control

When everything else feels out of control, our emotions, our relationships, our world, building a wall can feel like taking control back. It can feel empowering to say, "You won't hurt me again."

But let's not confuse control with healing.

Control says, "I'll never be vulnerable again." Healing says, "I'll learn to trust wisely."

Control says, "I don't need anyone." Healing says, "I can choose who is safe and who isn't."

Control says, "If I let you in, you'll break me." Healing says, "If I let myself heal, I'll be strong enough to love again."

Who Are You Without the Wall?

Have you asked yourself that? Who would you be without the sarcasm, the detachment, the guardedness? What kind of relationships would you attract if you let people see the real you? How different would your life be if you weren't afraid of being hurt?

This isn't about being reckless. It's not about tearing the wall down for anyone and everyone. It's about intentional healing. It's about learning how to discern, how to protect your peace without blocking your blessing.

Recognizing Your Wall

Sometimes we don't even realize how high our walls are. But you can usually tell by your behavior:

- Do you shut down when people get too close?
- Do you avoid deep conversations?
- Do you ghost people when they ask real questions?
- Do you pretend to be "unbothered" when you're actually hurting?
- Do you sabotage healthy relationships?

If any of that sounds familiar, your wall might be keeping you from the very healing you're praying for.

How to Start Taking the Wall Down

1. Acknowledge the pain that built it. Be honest about where the wall came from. Name the betrayal. Name the heartbreak. Don't minimize it. Don't rush past it. Sit with it.

2. Decide that healing matters more than hiding. You don't have to be fully healed to start. But you do have to be willing. Willing to do the work. Willing to trust again…first yourself, then others.

3. Choose safe people. Not everyone deserves access to your vulnerability. But there are people who do. Find them. Pray for them. Look for consistency, honesty, accountability.

4. Practice being seen. It doesn't have to be all at once. Share a little more. Open up a little more. Let someone in. It's okay to go slow. Healing has no timeline.

5. Have compassion for yourself. You built the wall because you needed it. That version of you was doing their best. But now, you're choosing something better. Be kind as you transition.

6. Replace isolation with intentional boundaries. A boundary says, "This is where I end and you begin." A wall says, "You're not allowed in at all." Choose boundaries. They protect without imprisoning.

When the Wall Comes Down...

You'll feel exposed. Vulnerable. Maybe even scared. But you'll also feel free. You'll feel what it's like to be known. To be loved for who you really are. To stop performing, pretending, protecting.

You'll start to see who's really there for you. You'll learn to say no without guilt and yes without fear. You'll rebuild your life not from behind a wall, but out in the open, where love can reach you.

Let's Be Really Real... Again

You can't keep asking God to heal you if you're not willing to open the door. You can't keep praying for healthy love while staying locked behind fear. You can't say you're tired of being alone while clinging to the wall that keeps people out.

At some point, you have to choose: Do I want to be safe, or do I want to be free? Because freedom requires risk. It requires trust. And trust requires healing.

The wall might have been your survival mechanism, but healing is your transformation.

You Are Worth the Risk

Loving again is a risk. Trusting again is a risk. Healing is a risk.

But you are worth that risk.

And when you start choosing connection over control, healing over hiding, vulnerability over fear…you'll see that the love, peace, and intimacy you've been praying for was always possible.

It just couldn't reach you through the wall.

The Wall

Reflection Questions:

1. What pain led you to build your wall?

2. What are you afraid will happen if you let your wall down?

3. In what ways has the wall protected you, and in what ways has it limited you?

4. Who in your life might be a safe place to start opening up?

5. How can you begin to practice vulnerability in small ways?

6. What boundaries do you need to put in place instead of walls?

Chapter Nine

Trust is Trust

Trust is Trust

Trust. It's a word we hear every day. It's something we expect in relationships, work environments, and even in the most mundane aspects of life. But have you ever stopped to ask yourself: What does trust really mean?

The dictionary defines trust simply as: "a firm belief in the reliability, truth, ability, or strength of someone or something." That's it. No frills. No exceptions. It's as clear as that. But what happens when we complicate it? What happens when we try to make trust something it's not, something that can bend, shift, or be manipulated?

The truth is simple, and sometimes simple truths are the hardest to swallow: Trust is trust. You either have it, or you don't. There is no middle ground. There's no such thing as "kinda trustworthy" or "halfway trustworthy." Either you trust, or you don't. Either you are trustworthy, or you're not.

The Power of Simple Truths

We often want to make trust into something more complex because it's uncomfortable to face the fact that it's a basic, straightforward principle. We want to add nuance and layers to make it easier to manipulate. We want to say things like, "I trust them most of the time, but sometimes they mess up." But that's not trust. That's not the definition.

The truth about trust is that it's an all-or-nothing concept. You can't half-trust someone and expect it to work. You can't say, "I trust them to do this, but not that," and expect the relationship to function in a healthy way. Either the person is trustworthy, or they aren't. And the same applies to you. Either you are trustworthy or you're not.

And here's where things get tricky for a lot of us. It's easy to look at someone else's actions and say, "I don't trust them anymore." But it's harder to turn that same lens on ourselves and ask, "Am I trustworthy?"

We want to blame others for the lack of trust we experience, but the truth is that trust isn't just a matter of others being trustworthy; it's about us being trustworthy as well.

Trust is a Two-Way Street

Trust isn't just about giving it to others; it's also about earning it from others. It's a relationship dynamic. If we want to be trusted, we have to be trustworthy.

Let's be honest, trust takes time. It's not something that just happens overnight. It's built through small actions, consistency, and a demonstrated reliability that shows others that you can be counted on.

When you break someone's trust, it takes time to rebuild it. No matter how many times you say, "I'm sorry," no matter how many excuses you offer, the only thing that truly rebuilds trust is your actions. The same goes for yourself. If you've broken your own trust, if you've repeatedly let yourself down, it's going to take time to rebuild that connection with yourself. But trust me, it is possible.

The Responsibility of Trust

One of the hardest truths we face in relationships, in business, in life, is that we are all responsible for the trust we give and receive. The way you handle trust speaks volumes about who you are. It's not just about you being trustworthy; it's about you being responsible with the trust others place in you.

When someone trusts you, they are giving you a piece of their heart, their vulnerability, and their faith in you. To mishandle that trust is to betray not just them, but yourself too. When you violate someone's trust, it doesn't just damage the relationship…it damages your ability to trust yourself. Because if you can't keep your promises to others, how can you trust yourself to make the right decisions?

How Trust is Built

Trust is built on consistency. It's not about grand gestures or flashy promises. It's about showing up, time and time again, with integrity. It's the little things. The moments when no one is watching, when the stakes aren't high, when the outcome doesn't affect your life in any significant way. That's when trust is built. It's in the small, unremarkable actions that accumulate into a mountain of credibility.

Here's an example: Imagine you've committed to something. Whether it's at work, in a relationship, or a personal goal. There's a difference between saying, "I'll get it done" and consistently showing up and following through. It's not about the words you say, but about your actions. Actions speak louder than words, and the more you show up and follow through, the more trust you build.

This applies to both external relationships and the relationship you have with yourself. If you're constantly breaking promises to yourself, you can't trust yourself. You're undermining your ability to rely on your own decisions and judgment.

What Happens When You Don't Trust?

If you're reading this and feeling like you're constantly struggling with trust issues, I want to ask you something: What happens when you don't trust?

When you don't trust others, you're essentially locking yourself in a cage. You're refusing to let people in, to open your heart, to experience vulnerability. You're keeping everyone at arm's length. And while that may feel safe in the short term, it's an isolation that slowly wears you down.

Not trusting others keeps you from building deep connections. It keeps you from experiencing true love, friendship, and collaboration. It creates barriers where there should be bridges. It creates resentment, doubt, and disconnection.

But what happens when you don't trust yourself?

Not trusting yourself is an even more dangerous game. When you don't trust your own decisions, your own instincts, and your own ability to make the right choices, you are paralyzed. You second-guess every decision. You become afraid to take risks. You put your life on hold, always waiting for someone else to make decisions for you because you don't trust your own judgment.

Self-doubt can rob you of your potential. It can keep you stuck in fear and confusion, never moving forward, always looking back and wondering "What if?"

Trust is Trust: No Shortcuts

There are no shortcuts when it comes to trust. It's not something you can negotiate or bend. It is what it is. You either trust, or you don't. Trust isn't conditional. It doesn't come with an asterisk that says, "Trust this person but only in certain situations." No, trust is absolute. It either exists, or it doesn't. And the same goes for being trustworthy. You can't be trustworthy just when it's convenient. You can't be partially trustworthy. It doesn't work that way.

I'm sure we've all heard the phrase, "Trust is earned." But let's take it a step further…trust is maintained. It's not a one-time thing. You earn trust over time, and you maintain it with every action, every decision, every word you speak. That's what it means to be trustworthy. It's not just about earning trust once; it's about showing up every single time, consistently proving that you can be counted on.

The Truth About Trust: It's Always There

Here's another important truth: Trust is not something you can turn on and off. It's not something you can compartmentalize. You can't say, "I trust this person, but I don't trust that person," and expect everything to be okay. Trust is a way of being. It's a way of living. You either choose to trust, or you choose not to.

The foundation of trust is built on belief. Trust is a firm belief in someone or something. And belief requires consistency. It's the same with the relationship you have with yourself. Do you believe in your ability to make good decisions? Do you believe that you deserve trust?

Trust Is Trust

You cannot function in a healthy, balanced life if you don't have a solid foundation of trust, both in others and in yourself. Trust is essential, and there is no workaround. You can't build meaningful connections, personal success, or emotional well-being without trust. It's the cornerstone of everything.

When it comes to building trust, both in others and in yourself, there are no shortcuts, no compromises. Trust is trust. It's either there, or it's not. And the only way to live a life free of fear, regret, and doubt is to build trust. Trust in others, but most importantly, trust in yourself.

Don't shy away from trusting. Don't hide behind your walls of protection. Trust is the foundation of every meaningful relationship, every breakthrough, and every moment of peace you will experience. When you learn to trust, you unlock the door to a fuller, richer life.

Trust is trust. And that is enough.

Reflection Questions

1. Where in my life am I trying to "half-trust" someone or something—and what is that really costing me?

2. Can I confidently say I am trustworthy?

3. Have I been mishandling someone's trust without realizing the damage it's causing?

4. Do I trust myself enough to follow through on my own promises?

5. What part of my life is suffering right now because I refuse to trust—whether it's others, God, or myself?

Trust Is Trust

Chapter Ten

Transparency: The Heart of Trust

Trust Issues

Transparency: The Heart of Trust

Trust is the foundation upon which all relationships. Personal, professional, and spiritual…are built. Without it, we find ourselves adrift, disconnected, and uncertain of who or what we can rely on. But trust is more than just a word. It's a feeling, an energy, and it's something that can be easily broken if not handled with care. What makes trust work? The ability to be transparent.

Transparency is a concept that many people misunderstand. I once heard someone say that omitting the truth was being honest. The idea behind this statement was that as long as you didn't outright lie, you were still in the realm of honesty. I beg to differ. Omitting the truth, withholding key information, or saying only what's comfortable for you to share isn't honesty, it's avoidance. It's fear. It's the coward's way out.

In reality, honesty doesn't work unless it's backed by transparency. Transparency means being open and forthright, no matter how uncomfortable it is. It means sharing your truth, your intentions, and your heart, even when you're unsure of how it will be received. Transparency is the cornerstone of trust, and without it, trust is fragile, easily broken, and difficult to rebuild.

The Role of Transparency in Trust

When you are transparent, you are not just showing someone the parts of yourself that are easy to show. You are unveiling the parts of yourself that are messy, complicated, and perhaps not always pretty. Being transparent means letting go of the fear that if people see the real you, they might leave or judge you. It's about being willing to expose yourself fully to the people you care about, without the need for self-protection.

Transparency isn't just about telling the truth, it's about showing the truth. It's about letting your actions, your words, and your intentions all align in a way that leaves no room for doubt. When you're transparent, there's no room for deception or misunderstanding. There's no guessing game. What you see is what you get.

Without transparency, trust becomes fragile. Think of it like a house built on a shaky foundation. It may stand for a while, but over time, cracks will begin to appear. It's the same in relationships. If someone is hiding parts of themselves or withholding important information, trust becomes difficult to build. Without transparency, we're left to fill in the gaps with assumptions and guesses. We're left wondering, "What aren't they telling me?" and, "What are they hiding?" These questions breed doubt, suspicion, and insecurity.

Why People Struggle with Transparency

For many, transparency is difficult. In fact, for some, it's terrifying. The thought of being vulnerable, of letting someone see you for who you really are, is a daunting prospect. We live in a world that values perfection, strength, and self-sufficiency. Showing our weaknesses, flaws, or mistakes can make us feel small or less-than. We fear rejection, judgment, or criticism.

But the truth is, transparency doesn't make you weak, it makes you strong. It takes courage to be open, to share your heart, and to be honest with others. It takes even more strength to be transparent with yourself. When you are honest with yourself, you stop hiding behind the walls you've built and start to confront your fears, insecurities, and past wounds. This is how healing begins.

Transparency requires vulnerability. It means opening yourself up, even when you're unsure of the outcome. It means exposing your deepest fears and desires without the promise of approval or acceptance. And while it can feel terrifying in the moment, it's the only way to foster real, deep, and lasting trust. Without it, relationships are shallow and unfulfilled.

The Difference Between Honesty and Transparency

Many people confuse honesty with transparency, but they are not the same thing. Honesty is a necessary part of transparency, but it doesn't encompass the full scope of what it means to be transparent.

Honesty is about telling the truth. It's about speaking what's factual, without distortion or fabrication. But honesty alone isn't enough. Someone can be honest with you and still hide important information, leave out key details, or give you only part of the story. This is what I mean when I say that omitting the truth is not being honest. It's being partial. It's being evasive.

Transparency, on the other hand, is about full disclosure. It's about saying what's on your mind and sharing what's in your heart. It's about offering the whole picture, not just the parts that are comfortable or easy to share. Transparency means that there are no hidden agendas, no ulterior motives, and no secrets. It's about aligning your actions with your words and ensuring that everything you do is in line with the truth.

The Benefits of Transparency in Relationships

There are many benefits to being transparent in your relationships. The first, and perhaps the most obvious, is that transparency fosters trust. When you are transparent, you give others the confidence that you are being truthful with them. There are no games, no confusion, and no room for doubt. When you trust someone enough to be transparent, you give them the freedom to trust you in return. This mutual trust creates a foundation of safety and security in the relationship.

Another benefit of transparency is that it allows for deeper connections. When you are transparent, you open the door for vulnerability. And vulnerability, as difficult as it may seem, is the gateway to intimacy. True intimacy can only exist when both people are open and honest with one another. When you share your true self, your fears, your struggles, and your hopes, you create space for the other person to do the same. This leads to a more authentic and meaningful relationship.

Transparency also promotes personal growth. When you are transparent with yourself, you are forced to confront your weaknesses, mistakes, and areas of growth. This is how you begin to heal and improve. Transparency helps you become more self-aware and more attuned to your own emotions, desires, and needs. It helps you learn from your mistakes and grow from them, rather than hiding from them.

Finally, transparency can reduce anxiety and stress. When you are transparent with others, you don't have to carry the burden of hiding your truth. You don't have to worry about being caught in a lie or keeping track of what you've said.

Instead, you can be at peace knowing that you are living in alignment with your values, and that your relationships are built on authenticity and trust.

How to Practice Transparency

If you've been hiding behind walls or avoiding full disclosure, becoming transparent can be a difficult process. But it's an essential step in building meaningful relationships and cultivating self-trust. Here are some steps to help you practice transparency:

1. Start with yourself – Transparency begins with self-awareness. You need to be honest with yourself about your feelings, desires, and fears. Take time to reflect on your inner world and acknowledge the parts of yourself that you've been hiding. When you can be transparent with yourself, you'll be able to share your truth with others more easily.

2. Communicate openly – Being transparent requires open communication. Don't be afraid to share what's on your mind, even if it's uncomfortable. Speak your truth with kindness and compassion, and be prepared to listen to the truth of others. Transparency isn't just about speaking; it's about creating an environment where open, honest communication can thrive.

3. Be vulnerable – Vulnerability is the key to transparency. It's about letting your guard down and allowing yourself to be seen for who you truly are. This may feel risky, but it's essential for deep connection. When you allow yourself to be vulnerable, you give others permission to do the same.

4. Set healthy boundaries – Transparency doesn't mean that you have to share every single detail of your life. You have the right to set boundaries and to protect your privacy. Being transparent is about sharing the right information at the right time, and ensuring that you are being open and honest without overexposing yourself.

5. Take responsibility for your actions – Transparency also means taking responsibility for your mistakes and your choices. When you make a mistake, own up to it. Be honest about what went wrong and take steps to make things right. This demonstrates integrity and accountability, which are crucial for building trust.

6. Practice consistency – Transparency isn't a one-time thing. It's something that you must practice consistently. Trust is built through repeated actions, and transparency is no different. Make transparency a habit in all areas of your life, and it will naturally strengthen your relationships and your self-trust.

The Risks of Transparency

While transparency has many benefits, it's important to acknowledge that it's not always easy. There are risks involved. When you are transparent, you open yourself up to judgment, criticism, and even rejection. Not everyone will appreciate your honesty, and some people may not be ready to accept your truth.

But the risks of transparency are far outweighed by the rewards. If you are authentic and transparent, you will attract people who value you for who you truly are, not for the mask you wear. Transparency allows you to build relationships based on trust, respect, and mutual understanding.

Embrace Transparency for a Trustworthy Life

In the end, transparency is the heart of trust. Without it, trust is shallow and fragile. When we practice transparency, we create space for authenticity, vulnerability, and connection. It's not always easy, but it's always worth it. By being transparent with others—and most importantly, with ourselves—we lay the foundation for deep, meaningful relationships and a life filled with trust.

Trust isn't something you can fake. It's built through transparency, consistency, and honesty. It's a process, not a destination. But when you embrace transparency, you unlock the power of trust to transform your relationships, your life, and your sense of self-worth.

Transparency: The Heart of Trust

Reflection Question

1. In what areas of your life have you mistaken honesty for true transparency?

2. What fears or insecurities keep you from being fully transparent with others?

3. How transparent are you with yourself about your own needs, mistakes, and patterns?

4. Who in your life deserves more transparency from you right now, and what's one step you can take toward that?

Chapter Eleven

Get Back to Trusting God

Get Back to Trusting God

Trusting God is a foundational principle in the journey of faith. It's one of the most powerful things we can do, yet it's often one of the hardest. For many of us, there are moments in life when our trust in God is shaken. The questions begin to swirl: Why didn't He show up when I needed Him? Why did He allow this hurt to happen? Why did He let me go through this pain?

If you're reading this, you might be facing one of those moments. Maybe you've experienced disappointment, loss, or unfulfilled expectations. Maybe you prayed for something with all your heart, but the outcome wasn't what you hoped for. The job didn't come through. The relationship fell apart. The illness didn't go away. And now, you're left wondering where God was in all of it.

Here's the truth: Just because things didn't happen the way we expected doesn't mean God has failed us. Trusting God doesn't mean that we get everything we want, or that life will always go according to our plans. It's about learning to trust His timing, His wisdom, and His love…even when life doesn't make sense. It's about returning to a place of faith, even when disappointment tries to pull us away.

The Struggle of Unmet Expectations

It's easy to trust God when everything is going right. When we're healthy, when our relationships are strong, when our finances are stable—it's easy to say, "God is good," and to believe that His plans are unfolding perfectly in our lives. But the true test of trust comes when life takes a turn that we didn't expect.

When something goes wrong, our natural instinct is often to question God. Why did He allow this to happen? Why didn't He stop it? Why didn't He intervene?

But God's ways are not our ways, and His thoughts are higher than our thoughts. His timing doesn't always align with ours, and His purposes are not always immediately clear. There are moments when the hurt and pain we experience are a part of His greater plan, a plan that we may not fully understand in the moment.

What we often fail to realize in these moments of struggle is that the very thing we're struggling with may be the catalyst for our growth. We may be facing a difficult season, but that doesn't mean God has abandoned us. It may be that He's using this season to shape us, to teach us, and to build our trust in Him. Sometimes, what looks like a setback is actually a setup for something greater.

God's Timing is Perfect

The key to getting back to trusting God lies in understanding that His timing is perfect. We are finite beings, limited by time and space. We see only a small part of the picture, and our perspective is clouded by our emotions, desires, and fears. But God sees the whole picture. He knows what is best for us, and He knows when the right time is for everything.

Trust Issues

In the Bible, we see countless examples of people who had to wait on God's timing. Abraham waited for years for the promise of a son, yet the fulfillment of that promise came at just the right time. Joseph was sold into slavery, falsely accused, and imprisoned, but he trusted God through it all, knowing that God had a plan for him. David was anointed king, yet he spent years running for his life before he took the throne. And in each of these stories, God's timing was perfect.

God's delays are not denials. Just because something hasn't happened yet doesn't mean it won't happen. It simply means that it's not the right time. We may not understand why we have to wait, but trusting God's timing means believing that He is in control, even when we can't see the way forward.

Where Did It Go Wrong?

There's a danger in losing trust in God, especially when life doesn't go the way we want. When things don't happen the way we hoped, we can easily slip into disappointment, doubt, and even bitterness. But this is where we need to be careful. When we allow our circumstances to dictate our trust in God, we're allowing our faith to be based on our own limited understanding.

We've all been there. We pray for something specific, with all our heart. We wait, and we wait. And then when it doesn't happen, we wonder: Why did God let me down? Why didn't He answer my prayer?

The problem is not that God let us down—it's that we placed our trust in a specific outcome, instead of trusting God's wisdom and sovereignty. We must understand that God's plans for us are always good, even when they don't align with our own desires. What feels like a disappointment in the moment could be the very thing that leads us to something better.

Shifting Our Perspective

One of the first steps in getting back to trusting God is shifting our perspective. Instead of focusing on what hasn't happened, we need to focus on what God has already done for us. He has brought us through countless trials before, and He hasn't failed us yet. He has been faithful, even when we couldn't see the way forward.

Trusting God means remembering that He is a good Father. It means knowing that He has our best interests at heart, even when things don't make sense. It's easy to trust God when life is going well, but real faith is built in the storm. It's in the moments of doubt, uncertainty, and pain that we must choose to trust Him all the more.

When life doesn't go as planned, it's an opportunity to grow deeper in our trust. It's an invitation to lean into God more fully, to seek His guidance, and to believe that He is still in control. Even when everything around us feels chaotic, we can trust that God is working behind the scenes for our good.

Getting Back to Trusting God

So how do we get back to trusting God when our faith has been shaken? Here are a few steps:

1. Acknowledge your feelings – It's okay to feel disappointed, hurt, or confused. Don't suppress your emotions or pretend that everything is fine. God knows what you're feeling, and He wants you to be honest with Him. Acknowledging your pain is the first step in healing.

2. Reflect on God's faithfulness – Take time to remember the ways God has been faithful in the past. Think about the times when He has come through for you, even when you didn't deserve it. This will help you regain perspective and remind you that God hasn't let you down before.

3. Release your expectations – Let go of the need for things to happen a certain way. Trust that God's plan is better than your own. Sometimes, what we think is best for us isn't actually what we need. Trust that God's timing is perfect, even if it's different from your own.

4. Pray and surrender – Spend time in prayer, not just asking for what you want, but surrendering your will to God. Trusting God means letting go of control and allowing Him to work in His timing. Pray for strength to trust, and for peace in the waiting.

5. Trust His character, not just His actions – Ultimately, trust is not about what God does for us, it's about who He is. God is faithful, loving, and good. Even when we don't understand what's happening in our lives, we can trust that His character is unchanging. He is always for us, always working on our behalf.

6. Choose faith over fear – When fear begins to creep in, choose to trust God instead. Faith is not the absence of fear, but the decision to trust God in spite of it. Choose to believe that God is in control, even when life feels out of control.

Trusting God in All Things

Trusting God is not always easy. It requires surrender, faith, and patience. But when we choose to trust Him, we are choosing to trust in His goodness, His timing, and His plan for

Get Back to Trusting God

our lives. God's plans for us are far greater than anything we could ever imagine, and when we align ourselves with His will,

we open ourselves up to blessings and growth that we never thought possible.

No matter what has happened in your life, no matter how long you've been waiting, remember that God has not abandoned you. His love for you is unchanging, and He is working in ways that you cannot see. Trust in His timing, trust in His faithfulness, and trust that He will always be there for you, no matter what.

Get back to trusting God…not just in the good times, but in the hard times too. Because when you trust in God, you can be confident that He will never let you down. His plans are always for your good, and His timing is always perfect. Trust Him today, and watch as He leads you into a future filled with hope, peace, and purpose.

Reflection Questions

1. Where has my trust in God been shaken, and why?
Take a moment to honestly reflect on a recent situation that caused you to doubt God's faithfulness. What did you expect to happen? How did it affect your faith? Write down your thoughts and be truthful with yourself and with God. Healing begins with honesty.

2. What are three ways God has shown up for me in the past?
Go back and remember. Recall times when God answered a prayer, provided for you, comforted you, or gave you strength when you didn't think you had any left. Write them down and thank Him. This practice strengthens your trust in His consistency.

3. Am I trusting outcomes or God Himself?
We often put our faith in *what we want* instead of *who God is*. Ask yourself: Am I frustrated because God didn't do what I wanted, or because I forgot who He is? Reflect on what it means to trust God's character rather than your personal timeline.

4. What is God teaching me in this waiting season?
Instead of viewing your current struggle as punishment or neglect, ask: *What am I learning? How am I growing?* Waiting is

not wasted when God is involved. Let this reflection help you shift from complaint to growth.

5. How can I practice trusting God today, even in a small way?
Maybe it's praying instead of worrying. Maybe it's releasing control over something you've been obsessing about. Maybe it's choosing peace when you could choose panic. Write down one action step that reflects trust—and do it.

Chapter Twelve

It's Okay to Abandon the Trust Issues

It's Okay to Abandon the Trust Issues

We've all been there. We've all carried those heavy, painful trust issues that haunt us and keep us trapped in cycles of hurt, disappointment, and fear. Trust issues seem to become a part of us, like a shield we carry with us everywhere we go. We wear them like armor, thinking they'll protect us from future pain. But in reality, they only weigh us down, stop us from moving forward, and keep us from living the abundant life God has promised us.

At some point in our journey, we have to realize that it's okay to abandon those trust issues. It's okay to let go of the pain, the bitterness, and the fear that we've been holding onto for far too long. God has so much greater in store for you, and He's waiting for you to lay those trust issues down so He can lead you into a future filled with peace, hope, and healing.

Trust Issues: A Weight We Were Never Meant to Carry

It's easy to get caught up in the idea that our trust issues are something we must carry forever. We convince ourselves that they're part of our identity, that the hurt we've experienced from others is something we can never truly move past. But the reality is that trust issues are not meant to define us. They are not meant to hold us captive.

When we carry trust issues, we are essentially living in fear. We fear being hurt again, we fear disappointment, and we fear vulnerability. And while it's understandable to have these fears after experiencing betrayal or hurt, we cannot allow them to define our future. Carrying trust issues is like holding onto a chain that is anchored to our past. The more we hold onto those issues, the more they keep us bound to the pain we've experienced.

But here's the thing: God did not create us to live in bondage. We were not designed to carry the weight of hurt, anger, and distrust. That's why Jesus came, to set us free from the chains that bind us. And one of the first steps to freedom is realizing that it's okay to abandon our trust issues. We don't have to hold onto them any longer.

The Spiritual and Emotional Cost of Holding On

When we hold onto trust issues, we're not just holding onto the pain of the past, we're also preventing ourselves from experiencing the fullness of what God has for us. These issues can slowly drain us spiritually, emotionally, and even physically.

Spiritually, we may find ourselves distant from God. Our ability to fully trust Him becomes impaired because we've allowed our experiences with others to shape our view of Him. We start to believe that if people have let us down, God will do the same. And the more we believe this, the harder it becomes to surrender to Him, to truly trust Him with our lives.

Emotionally, trust issues can prevent us from building healthy, meaningful relationships. We may push people away, thinking that no one can be trusted. Or we may stay in toxic relationships, convinced that we're not worthy of something better. We may avoid vulnerability altogether, keeping our hearts locked up and closed off from others.

Physically, the weight of carrying trust issues can manifest in stress, anxiety, and even physical illness. The constant worry and fear about being hurt or betrayed again takes a toll on our bodies. It can keep us up at night, make our hearts race, and cause a sense of unease that never quite goes away.

All of this—spiritual, emotional, and physical damage—is the result of holding onto something that was never meant to be ours to carry. Trust issues can feel like a heavy burden, and as long as we carry them, we will never experience the fullness of peace, joy, and freedom that God has for us.

The Power of Letting Go

Letting go of trust issues doesn't mean that we forget about the pain or the hurt we've experienced. It doesn't mean that we pretend everything is fine when it's not. Letting go of trust issues means choosing to release the hold that those issues have over us. It means deciding that we no longer want to be defined by the betrayals and disappointments of our past. It means choosing to heal and to move forward.

The act of letting go requires us to do a few things:

1. Acknowledge the pain – We cannot heal from what we refuse to acknowledge. In order to let go of our trust issues, we first need to acknowledge the pain and the hurt that they've caused. We need to give ourselves permission to feel that pain, to grieve, and to process it. Only then can we begin to heal.

2. Forgive – Forgiveness is a key part of letting go of trust issues. We must forgive those who have hurt us, not because

they deserve it, but because we deserve peace. Holding onto unforgiveness only keeps us stuck in the past, tied to the pain of betrayal. Forgiveness is not a one-time event, it's a decision we make daily, choosing to release the bitterness and anger that keep us bound.

3. Release the need for control – Trust issues often stem from a deep need for control. We want to protect ourselves from future hurt, so we try to control everything around us. But the truth is, we can't control other people's actions or the outcomes of our lives. Letting go of trust issues means surrendering control to God, trusting that He knows what's best for us and that He will guide us through every situation.

4. Choose to trust again – Letting go of trust issues means choosing to trust again, even when it feels risky. It means deciding that we won't allow the pain of the past to prevent us from embracing the love, joy, and peace that God has for us. We choose to trust God first and foremost, knowing that He is the only one who will never fail us.

Spiritual Death from Holding On

The danger of holding onto trust issues is that they don't just affect our relationships with others, they also affect our relationship with God. When we allow trust issues to take root in our hearts, we can slowly begin to die spiritually.

It's easy to get frustrated and angry with God when things don't go our way. We may question His goodness, His faithfulness, and His timing. We may even feel like He has let us down. But this is the lie that trust issues feed us: the belief that

God is not trustworthy, that He is not good, and that He has abandoned us.

When we believe this lie, we begin to withdraw from God. We stop praying, stop seeking Him, and stop trusting Him. And over time, we begin to wither spiritually. We may still go through the motions: attending church, reading our Bibles, but our hearts are far from Him.

This is why it's so important to abandon our trust issues. When we hold onto them, we are essentially choosing to live in spiritual death. But when we choose to let go, to trust God again, we allow ourselves to experience the fullness of His love and grace. We open ourselves up to spiritual growth, to a deeper relationship with Him, and to a life of peace and joy that only He can provide.

Breaking Free from the Cycle of Hurt

Trust issues can feel like an endless cycle. We get hurt, we shut ourselves off, we build walls, and we vow never to trust again. But this cycle will only continue until we choose to break it. The longer we hold onto our trust issues, the longer we delay the healing that God wants to bring into our lives.

God has so much greater for you. He has a life of peace, joy, and freedom waiting for you, but it's up to you to let go of the trust issues that are holding you back. When you choose to abandon them, you're choosing to step into the future that God has for you. You're choosing to trust again, not just in others, but in Him.

It's Okay to Abandon the Trust Issues

You Were Made for More

God created you for more than living in the shadows of hurt, fear, and distrust. He created you for a life of wholeness,

purpose, and freedom. But you cannot experience that life if you continue to carry the weight of trust issues.

The moment you decide to let go, to trust again, is the moment you begin to walk into your true purpose. God wants to use your pain for good. He wants to take the hurt you've experienced and turn it into something beautiful. But He cannot do that if you continue to hold onto the past.

Trusting God Again

The first step in abandoning your trust issues is trusting God again. It's about believing that He is good, that He is faithful, and that He will never let you down. Trusting God means surrendering your fears, your doubts, and your pain to Him, knowing that He will carry it for you.

When you trust God, you can begin to trust others again. You can build relationships without fear of betrayal. You can love without hesitation. You can live a life of peace and freedom because you know that God is always with you, guiding you, protecting you.

It's okay to abandon your trust issues. It's okay to let go of the hurt, the bitterness, and the fear that you've been holding onto for so long. God has so much more for you. Don't let the trust issues of your past keep you from the abundant life that God has for you.

Let go of the weight. Trust God again. And step into the future He has waiting for you.

Reflection Questions

1. **What specific trust issues have you been holding onto, and how have they affected your relationship with God and others?**
   Take time to identify the roots of your distrust. Reflect on how these issues have shaped your decisions, your faith, and your emotional well-being.

2. **What would it look like for you to let go of those trust issues today?**
   Imagine the freedom and peace that could come if you surrendered them to God. What emotions does that thought stir in you—fear, hope, hesitation?

3. **Who do you need to forgive in order to move forward—and are you willing to do it?**
   Forgiveness is a key part of healing. Consider the people or situations that have deeply hurt you. What's keeping you from forgiving them?

4. **How have your trust issues influenced your view of God's character?**
   Be honest with yourself. Have your past experiences with people distorted your ability to trust God fully? What would it take to realign your view of Him with His Word?

5. **What steps can you take this week to begin trusting again —starting with God?**
Healing doesn't happen overnight, but it does begin with intentional action. Write down one practical thing you can do to begin the process of healing and rebuilding trust.

Trust Issues

Chapter Thirteen

How Can I Enhance My Trust in God

How Can I Enhance My Trust in God

Trust is one of the cornerstones of our relationship with God. Yet, as we navigate the complexities of life, we often find ourselves struggling to fully trust in Him. Whether we've experienced personal setbacks, losses, or disappointments, it can be difficult to maintain unwavering faith in God's plan. But the truth is, God is trustworthy. His love for us is unchanging, and His plans for us are good, even when we can't always see the bigger picture.

Enhancing your trust in God is not an overnight process; it's a journey, a lifelong commitment to growing deeper in your faith and understanding of who God is. In this chapter, we'll explore how you can enhance your trust in God and build a stronger, more intimate relationship with Him.

1. Acknowledge His Faithfulness in the Past

One of the best ways to enhance your trust in God is to look back and reflect on His faithfulness in your life. Reflecting on the times He has come through for you, even when you didn't know how things would turn out, can serve as a powerful reminder of His goodness. When we remember how He has always been there for us, it strengthens our belief that He will continue to be faithful in the future.

- **Reflect on past blessings**: Think about the times when God has provided for you, protected you, and answered your prayers. Even when things didn't go the way you expected, God's presence in those moments was evidence of His care and love for you.

- **Write down your testimonies**: One practical way to remember His faithfulness is by writing down your experiences of God's faithfulness. Keep a journal of the ways He has worked in your life. When doubts arise, revisit these testimonies to remind yourself of God's ability to come through.

Psalm 77:11-12 NIV says, "*I will remember the deeds of the Lord; yes, I will remember your miracles of long ago. I will consider all your works and meditate on all your mighty deeds.*" Reflecting on His past faithfulness fuels trust in His future provision.

2. Immerse Yourself in His Word

God's Word is full of promises, and one of the best ways to strengthen your trust in God is by diving deep into Scripture. The Bible reveals God's character, His heart for us, and His unwavering faithfulness. As you immerse yourself in His Word, you become more confident in His ability to handle every situation in your life.

- **Read the promises of God**: From the Old Testament to the New Testament, God has made promises to His people—promises of His love, His protection, His provision, and His guidance. The more you read and internalize these promises, the more you will grow in confidence and trust in Him.

- **Memorize Scripture**: Memorizing verses that speak about trust, faith, and God's character can serve as a tool to remind you of His truth in times of doubt. Scriptures like Proverbs 3:5-6

NIV, *"Trust in the Lord with all your heart and lean not on your own understanding,"* can help keep your mind and heart anchored in faith when challenges arise.

Joshua 1:9 NIV encourages us: *"Have I not commanded you? Be strong and courageous. Do not be afraid; do not be discouraged, for the Lord your God will be with you wherever you go."* Trusting in God's Word helps us to remember that He is with us in every circumstance.

3. Cultivate a Heart of Prayer

Trusting God is often rooted in our communication with Him. Prayer is not just about asking for things; it's about building a relationship with God, expressing our fears, desires, gratitude, and praises to Him. Through prayer, we are invited to hand over our burdens and trust that He will handle them.

- **Talk to God regularly**: Make time to communicate with God in your daily life. Share your heart with Him and allow space for His guidance. Prayer isn't just a monologue, it's a conversation. And the more you converse with God, the more you'll learn to trust His voice and His timing.

- **Pray about everything**: Don't hold back any area of your life from God. Trust Him with the small things, the big things, and everything in between. God cares about every aspect of your life and desires to walk with you through every moment.

Philippians 4:6-7 NIV reminds us: *"Do not be anxious about anything, but in every situation, by prayer and petition, with thanksgiving, present your requests to God. And the peace of God, which transcends all understanding, will guard your hearts and your minds in Christ Jesus."*

4. Surrender Your Will to God

One of the key aspects of trusting God is surrendering our own will and desires to Him. Trust is not about controlling every aspect of our lives but about yielding to God's perfect will, even when we don't fully understand it. Surrender means giving up the illusion of control and embracing the fact that God's ways are higher than ours.

- **Let go of control**: If you're someone who struggles with control, trusting God may feel especially difficult. But true trust is recognizing that you don't have to figure everything out on your own. Let go of the need to control your circumstances and allow God to work in His perfect timing.

- **Embrace God's will, not your own**: Surrendering means trusting that God's plan for your life is better than your own. Sometimes this means saying "yes" to things you didn't plan or "no" to things you thought you wanted. Trust that God is leading you to the place you are meant to be.

Jesus modeled perfect trust and surrender to the Father when He prayed in the Garden of Gethsemane, "*Not my will, but yours be done*" (Luke 22:42 NIV). His willingness to surrender His will to God resulted in the salvation of the world. Surrendering to God doesn't mean weakness; it means strength in trusting His sovereignty.

5. Spend Time in Worship

Worship is an intimate expression of our love for God and a way to acknowledge His greatness. Worship refocuses our hearts on the majesty and holiness of God, reminding us of His goodness and faithfulness. The more we worship God, the more our trust in Him is nurtured.

- **Worship in the good and the bad**: It's easy to worship when things are going well, but trust is truly enhanced when we worship in the midst of difficulties. Praise God even when it feels hard; He is still worthy, and worship aligns our hearts with His truth.

- **Sing songs that declare His faithfulness**: Music has a unique way of penetrating the soul. Find worship songs that speak to your situation and sing them out loud. Let the truth of God's faithfulness resonate in your spirit, and watch how your trust in Him grows.

Psalm 9:10 *NIV* says, *"Those who know your name trust in you, for you, Lord, have never forsaken those who seek you."* Worship deepens our understanding of God's name, His character, and His presence in our lives.

6. Embrace Patience in the Waiting

Sometimes our trust in God is tested by the waiting periods in life. Whether it's waiting for answers to prayers, waiting for clarity in a decision, or waiting for a breakthrough, these seasons of waiting can either strengthen or weaken our trust. How we handle the wait is crucial in enhancing our trust in God.

- **Trust God's timing**: We live in a culture that values immediacy and fast results, but God's timing is perfect. Even when it feels like nothing is happening, God is always at work behind the scenes. Trust that He is preparing you for something greater, and that His timing is better than yours.

- **Be patient with yourself**: Trusting God doesn't mean being perfect. Allow yourself grace during seasons of doubt. It's okay to wrestle with trust. It's okay to question, as long as you return to God with an open heart and a willingness to grow.

Isaiah 40:31 *NIV* promises, *"But those who hope in the Lord will renew their strength. They will soar on wings like eagles; they will run and not grow weary, they will walk and not be faint."* Trusting God's timing allows you to find rest and strength in the waiting.

7. Surround Yourself with a Community of Believers

Trusting God is not meant to be a solitary endeavor. We were created for community, and sometimes our trust in God is enhanced when we are surrounded by others who can encourage and support us in our faith journey.

- **Find accountability**: Surround yourself with people who encourage you to trust God, pray with you, and speak truth into your life. Sometimes, we need others to remind us of God's promises and to help us refocus our eyes on Him when doubt creeps in.

- **Share your struggles**: It's okay to admit when you're struggling with trust. Sharing your doubts with fellow believers can help you feel supported, and you'll likely find that they have walked through similar challenges. This shared experience builds trust in God as you encourage one another.

Proverbs 27:17 *NIV* says, *"As iron sharpens iron, so one person sharpens another."* A community of believers can help sharpen and strengthen our trust in God.

A Lifelong Journey of Trust

Enhancing your trust in God is not a one-time decision, it's a lifelong process. As you immerse yourself in His Word, surrender your will, pray, worship, and embrace the journey, you'll find your trust in God growing stronger. Trusting God is about choosing to believe that He is good, even when life doesn't make sense. It's about choosing to believe that He will never fail you, no matter what happens.

As you enhance your trust in God, remember that you are not alone. He is with you every step of the way, guiding you, strengthening you, and leading you into a life of peace, purpose, and joy.

Reflection Questions

1. When you look back on your life, what are three specific moments when God showed His faithfulness, even if it wasn't in the way you expected?

2. Which scripture about trust speaks most deeply to you right now, and why?

3. What areas of your life do you still find hardest to surrender to God's timing and plan?

4. How can prayer and worship become more natural parts of your daily rhythm, not just in crisis moments?

5. Who in your life can you lean on for accountability and encouragement when your faith feels shaky?

Chapter Fourteen

When My Past Trust Meets the New Me

When My Past Trust Meets the New Me

Trust isn't just a fleeting emotion. It's a foundation upon which relationships, peace, and healing are built. For many of us, trust feels like something we once had, something we lost along the way. Whether through the betrayal of others or the self-betrayal we've caused ourselves, trust can seem like a distant memory. But here's the good news: trust doesn't have to stay in the past.

When your past trust meets the new version of you—the one that's stronger, wiser, and more confident—you come to realize that you don't have to stay stuck in the trust battles you fought in previous seasons. You can choose to rebuild, to grow, and to become someone who stands in trust, no matter the circumstances. You've become whole. You've become healed. You've become stronger. And in this chapter, we will explore what happens when your new self encounters the brokenness of the past and learns to trust again.

1. Understanding the Impact of Past Trust Issues

Before we can embrace a new version of trust, we have to first acknowledge the impact that past trust issues have had on us. It's easy to want to avoid the pain, to push it down, to pretend it didn't happen. But the reality is that past hurts, broken relationships, and shattered trust shape who we are today.

- **Acknowledging the pain**: The first step in this journey is facing the truth of what has happened. The betrayals, the heartbreaks, the moments when someone else's actions or even your own led to a breakdown of trust…those are real. It's crucial to allow yourself to feel the pain and recognize how it impacted your ability to trust.

- **Recognizing the patterns:** Often, trust issues are rooted in patterns—whether from childhood, past relationships, or experiences that have made us wary of others. These patterns can hold us back from moving forward, leaving us stuck in cycles of doubt, fear, and suspicion. But recognizing these patterns allows us to break free.

Psalms 34:18 *NIV* says, *"The Lord is close to the brokenhearted and saves those who are crushed in spirit."* Trusting in God's healing power begins with acknowledging the brokenness and the fact that you don't have to stay there.

2. Embracing the New You

The moment your past trust issues meet the new version of you is transformative. As you grow, learn, and heal, you begin to see yourself as someone capable of trusting again. This new version of yourself is resilient. You've been through the fire and come out stronger. You've learned from your mistakes, and most importantly, you've realized that you are worthy of trust… both from others and from yourself.

- **Recognizing your growth**: Take a moment to look back on how far you've come. You're not the person you were a year ago, a month ago, or even a week ago. Growth takes time, and as you learn from your past, you develop a stronger sense of self. You begin to see your worth, your value, and your ability to trust again.

- **Becoming healthier**: As you heal, you become more equipped to handle the emotional weight of trust. You've learned to set boundaries, to protect your peace, and to take care of your mental and emotional health. Trust, after all, isn't just about others, it's about trusting yourself to make healthy decisions for your own well-being.

- **Embracing your wisdom**: With every painful experience comes wisdom. The wisdom you've gained from overcoming your past trust issues is invaluable. You know now when to speak up and when to walk away. You know when to give second chances and when to let go. You've become wiser in how you approach trust, both with others and with God.

Ephesians 4:22-24 *NIV* encourages us: *"You were taught, with regard to your former way of life, to put off your old self, which is being corrupted by its deceitful desires; to be made new in the attitude of your minds; and to put on the new self, created to be like God in true righteousness and holiness."* This new self is marked by the ability to trust without being naïve, to be open to relationships without fear, and to face the future with confidence.

3. Recognizing Your Worth and Ability to Trust Again

For many of us, the hardest part of trusting again is the belief that we are worthy of that trust. When we've been let down in the past, it's easy to internalize that hurt and believe we are unworthy of anything better. But the truth is, your worth has never been defined by the actions of others.

- **Trusting yourself**: The foundation of trust begins within. Learning to trust yourself again means recognizing that you are capable of making wise decisions and handling life's challenges. You've proven to yourself that you can heal, that you can grow, and that you can move forward. Trusting yourself is essential in building a future where trust doesn't feel like a risk, but a blessing.

- **Trusting others**: Once you've rebuilt your trust in yourself, it becomes easier to trust others. You no longer carry the weight of past betrayals with you into every new relationship. Instead, you approach trust with a sense of security in who you are. You can open your heart and give others the opportunity to show that they are worthy of your trust without feeling the need to protect yourself from every possible hurt.

Isaiah 43:1 NIV reminds us, "*But now, this is what the Lord says—he who created you, Jacob, he who formed you, Israel: 'Do not fear, for I have redeemed you; I have summoned you by name; you are mine.'*" You are worthy of trust because God has made you His own.

4. Understanding That Healing Is a Process, Not an Event

Trust is not something that can be rebuilt overnight. It's a process, a journey that requires time, patience, and intentional effort. Even with the newfound strength, wisdom, and health, it's important to recognize that healing takes time.

- **Allowing time for healing**: Don't rush the process. Trusting again doesn't mean that the scars from the past disappear instantly. It means acknowledging the scars but choosing to live in the present and future with a new perspective. Allow yourself the grace to heal at your own pace.

- **Embracing imperfection**: Trust is a messy, imperfect process. You may find yourself wavering at times, questioning whether you're doing the right thing or making the right decision. That's okay. Trusting again is not about perfection; it's about taking one step at a time, knowing that God is guiding your steps.

Philippians 1:6 *NIV* reassures us, *"Being confident of this, that he who began a good work in you will carry it on to completion until the day of Christ Jesus."* Trusting God's process in your life means giving Him the room to finish the work He's begun in you.

5. Choosing to Let Go of the Past

The old you, the one who struggled with trust, has had its time. But now it's time to let go of those old narratives and step into the new version of yourself. You are not defined by your past trust issues or the pain that you've experienced. You are defined by who God says you are…a beloved child, capable of trust, and worthy of love.

- **Forgiving those who hurt you**: Part of letting go of the past is forgiving those who have betrayed your trust. This doesn't mean you condone their actions or allow them to hurt you again. Forgiveness is about freeing yourself from the power their betrayal has over you. It's about choosing peace over bitterness, healing over holding on to the past.

- **Forgiving yourself**: Sometimes, the hardest person to forgive is yourself. Maybe you feel like you were responsible for some of the trust issues or that you should have known better. But you've learned, you've grown, and you're no longer that person. Letting go of self-blame allows you to embrace your new self with grace and confidence.

Isaiah 43:18-19 *NIV* encourages us, *"Forget the former things; do not dwell on the past. See, I am doing a new thing! Now it springs up; do you not perceive it? I am making a way in the wilderness and streams in the wasteland."* God is doing a new thing in your life, and the past no longer has to define your future.

6. Trusting in God's Greater Plan

Ultimately, when your past trust meets the new version of you, it's important to remember that your trust is rooted in something much greater than yourself. It's rooted in God's plan for your life. No matter the brokenness, no matter the pain, God's purpose for you is greater than any betrayal or hurt you've experienced.

- **Trusting in His timing**: God's timing is perfect. While the process of rebuilding trust may feel slow or painful, trust that God is orchestrating every detail of your life according to His good and perfect will. He is at work in your heart, making you stronger, wiser, and more equipped to handle the relationships and opportunities that come your way.

- **Trusting in His promises**: God has made promises to you; promises of peace, provision, healing, and restoration. As you walk through life, trusting that He is working everything out for your good, you can rest in the certainty that you will not be abandoned, and you will not be let down.

Romans 8:28 *NIV* reminds us, "*And we know that in all things God works for the good of those who love him, who have been called according to his purpose.*" Trusting in God's greater plan allows us to move forward with confidence, knowing that He is in control.

Trust as a New Beginning

When your past trust meets the new you, you realize that trust is not something to fear. It's not a risk; it's an opportunity for growth, healing, and new beginnings. You've become someone who is not defined by the scars of the past but by the strength and wisdom you've gained through the journey. And as you embrace trust again, you do so with the knowledge that you are capable, you are worthy, and you are never alone.

God is with you, and His plan for your life is filled with hope and promise. As you trust again, remember that your past doesn't have to control your future. Your trust is no longer rooted in the pain of what has been; it's rooted in the strength and peace of who you've become, and who God is still shaping you to be.

Reflection Questions

1. What past experiences have most shaped your struggles with trust, and how do you see those patterns showing up today?

2. How has God been growing the "new you" in this season, and where do you see evidence of healing?

3. What does it look like to forgive yourself fully for the choices or mistakes that damaged trust?

4. How can you remind yourself daily that your worth is not defined by betrayal or brokenness but by God's truth?

5. What practical steps can you take to release the old narratives and step boldly into your new self?

Chapter Fifteen

Trusting the Journey: Embracing Uncertainty with Faith

Trusting the Journey: Embracing Uncertainty with Faith

In a world filled with constant change, shifting expectations, and unpredictable circumstances, one of the most challenging aspects of trust is learning to trust the journey itself. It's not enough to just trust people or even ourselves; sometimes, we have to trust the process, the unfolding of events, and the journey that God has set before us...even when it doesn't look the way we thought it would.

Trusting the journey isn't about having all the answers, knowing the outcome, or feeling secure in every decision. It's about learning to walk by faith, even when the path ahead is unclear. It's about holding onto the truth that God is guiding you, even in moments of doubt, confusion, or uncertainty. In this chapter, we'll explore the importance of trusting the journey and embracing the unknown with confidence, patience, and faith.

1. The Challenge of Uncertainty

Uncertainty is one of the hardest things to face. We're conditioned to seek control, to plan, and to predict. We want to know what's coming next. We want to feel secure in the choices we make. But the reality of life is that not everything is predictable, and not every path is clear.

- **The discomfort of the unknown**: The unknown often brings discomfort, fear, and anxiety. When we don't know what lies ahead, it's easy to feel insecure or unsure of our choices. We might question ourselves, wondering if we're on the right path. The fear of the unknown can paralyze us, preventing us from taking steps forward.

- **The need for control**: Many of us struggle with the need to control our circumstances. We want to know how everything will turn out, and we want to make sure we're not making any mistakes. But true trust requires letting go of the illusion of control. It means acknowledging that we can't always dictate the outcome, but we can trust the One who holds our future.

Proverbs 3:5-6 NIV teaches us, *"Trust in the Lord with all your heart and lean not on your own understanding; in all your ways submit to him, and he will make your paths straight."* Trusting the journey means acknowledging that we don't have to have all the answers. We simply need to trust God's guidance.

2. Trusting God in the Midst of Uncertainty

At the core of trusting the journey is trust in God's plan. When we face uncertainty, it's easy to focus on our fears or the unknowns. But when we trust God, we can find peace even in the midst of chaos. Trusting the journey means believing that God is always at work, even when we can't see it.

- **Trusting His timing**: God's timing is often different from our own. We might want answers right now, but God knows exactly when the right moment is for us. Trusting His timing means surrendering our desire for immediate results and waiting patiently for Him to reveal the next step.

- **Trusting His plan**: God has a purpose for every season of life, even the ones that feel uncertain or difficult. Trusting the journey means believing that every step, every challenge, and every unexpected turn is part of God's greater plan for us.

Romans 8:28 *NIV* reminds us, *"And we know that in all things God works for the good of those who love him, who have been called according to his purpose."* Even when things don't make sense, we can trust that God is working everything out for our good.

3. Embracing the Process

Trusting the journey means embracing the process, not just the destination. It's easy to focus on the end result and forget that growth happens along the way. Every step, every lesson, and every challenge contributes to our growth and transformation.

- **Growth through adversity**: Sometimes, the journey is difficult. There are times when things don't go as planned, and it feels like everything is falling apart. But these are the moments when God often does His greatest work in us. Trusting the journey means embracing the adversity as part of the process, knowing that it's shaping us into the people we were meant to be.

- **Learning to be patient**: Patience is a vital part of the journey. We live in a world that demands instant results, but spiritual growth and transformation take time. Trusting the journey means learning to be patient with the process, allowing ourselves to grow at the pace God has set for us.

- **Celebrating small victories**: Along the way, there are often small victories that we overlook. We might be focused on the bigger picture, the future outcome, and forget to celebrate the progress we've made. Trusting the journey means acknowledging the steps we've taken, no matter how small, and celebrating the progress that's been made.

James 1:2-4 *NIV* encourages us, *"Consider it pure joy, my brothers and sisters, whenever you face trials of many kinds, because you know that the testing of your faith produces perseverance. Let perseverance finish its work so that you may be mature and complete, not lacking anything."* Every step in the process is shaping us into something better.

4. Trusting God to Lead Us Through the Wilderness

There are seasons in life when we feel like we're walking through a wilderness—a place of uncertainty, hardship, and confusion. It can feel like we're lost or stuck. But even in these seasons, we must trust that God is leading us. Trusting the journey means acknowledging that even in the wilderness, God is with us.

- **God's presence in the wilderness**: In the Bible, the wilderness was often a place of testing and growth. It was in the wilderness that the Israelites learned to trust God completely. When we're in our own wilderness seasons, we must remember that God is still with us, guiding us and providing for us. We don't have to fear the wilderness; it's often where God does some of His most profound work in us.

- **Learning to rely on God**: The wilderness teaches us to rely on God like never before. It strips away our self-sufficiency and reminds us that we cannot do it alone. Trusting the journey means leaning into God's strength, trusting that He will provide for our needs and guide us through the toughest times.

Psalm 23:4 *NIV* assures us, *"Even though I walk through the darkest valley, I will fear no evil, for you are with me; your rod and your staff, they comfort me."* God's presence is the greatest comfort in the wilderness.

5. Letting Go of the Need for Perfection

Part of trusting the journey is letting go of the need for everything to be perfect. We can spend so much time trying to control every detail, trying to make sure everything goes according to plan. But the truth is, perfection is impossible, and the pursuit of it only leads to frustration and exhaustion.

- **Embracing imperfection:** Trusting the journey means accepting that things won't always go as planned. There will be setbacks, mistakes, and detours. But these are part of the journey. Instead of striving for perfection, we can focus on learning, growing, and becoming better along the way.

- **Freedom from expectations**: Sometimes, we place unrealistic expectations on ourselves and others. We expect everything to fall into place, and when it doesn't, we feel like failures. Trusting the journey means freeing ourselves from these expectations and allowing God to shape our path as He sees fit.

Matthew 6:34 *NIV* reminds us, *"Therefore do not worry about tomorrow, for tomorrow will worry about itself. Each day has enough trouble of its own."* Trusting the journey means living in the present moment, without the pressure of trying to control everything.

6. Trusting God to Bring You Through the Unknown

At the heart of trusting the journey is trust in God to bring us through the unknown. We don't know what tomorrow will hold, but we do know that God is already there. He is with us in every step, guiding us, protecting us, and walking with us through the unknown.

- **Walking by faith**: Trusting the journey requires faith! Faith that God will guide us, even when we don't know where we're going. It's easy to trust when we can see the road ahead, but trusting in God's direction when we can't see the way takes courage and belief that He is in control.

- **Overcoming fear**: Fear often stands in the way of trusting the journey. We fear what might happen, what we might lose, or what we might not understand. But when we trust God, we can let go of that fear and move forward with confidence, knowing that He is leading us every step of the way.

Proverbs 16:9 *NIV* says, *"In their hearts humans plan their course, but the Lord establishes their steps."* Trusting the journey means believing that God is establishing our steps, even when we can't see the path ahead.

Trusting the Journey with Confidence

Trusting the journey isn't about having all the answers or knowing exactly what will happen. It's about walking with God, trusting that He is leading us, and embracing the uncertainty with faith. Life's journey may not always be easy, but when we trust God with the process, we can find peace, hope, and strength in the unknown. So trust the journey. Trust that God has a plan for your life, and trust that He will bring you through every season of uncertainty, guiding you toward His perfect will.

Reflection Questions

1. Where in your life right now are you most wrestling with uncertainty or the unknown?

2. How does the desire to control outcomes interfere with your ability to trust God's timing?

3. What lessons from past "wilderness seasons" can you carry into your current or future struggles?

4. What small victories on your journey do you need to pause and celebrate today?

5. How can you reframe your perspective on trials so that you see them as part of God's refining process instead of setbacks?

Chapter Sixteen

Did You Do It? Well, Own It

Did You Do It? Well, Own It

Let's just sit down and have this conversation...just you and me. No fluff, no pretense. I want to talk about something that most people run from. Something that takes real strength to admit.

Sometimes... it was you.

Yeah, I said it. Sometimes, it was me. We caused the distrust. We were the reason someone now guards their heart. We were the ones who couldn't be counted on. And if nobody has told you before, let me be the first—it's okay to admit that. Actually, it's necessary.

You cannot truly heal until you admit the part you played. You can't grow into a trustworthy person if you won't face the moments you weren't one. And you can't keep blaming everybody else when deep down, you know you created damage that you now wish you could undo.

Let's be real together.

No More Hiding Behind the Victim Card

Look, I get it. It's easier to talk about the hurt that was done to you than it is to talk about the hurt you caused others. We love playing the victim because it makes us feel safe. It takes the pressure off. It shifts the spotlight.

But at some point, you gotta stop. You gotta take that victim card, put it down on the table, and say, "I'm not playing this anymore."

Because here's the truth: you don't get to keep saying "people can't be trusted" if you've been the one breaking trust. You don't get to cry foul when the pain you feel is the same pain you caused. That's not healing. That's hiding. That's avoiding the truth.

And truth is the only path to real freedom.

Real Talk: You Knew What You Were Doing

We don't like to admit it, but a lot of the time, we knew. Maybe we were hurting. Maybe we felt ignored. Maybe we had our own trauma we hadn't dealt with yet. But we still knew. And we chose to move the way we did anyway.

- You knew lying would break their heart, but you did it to avoid the consequences.

- You knew ghosting would leave them confused, but you couldn't face the discomfort.

- You knew your actions were triggering, but you played it off like they were too sensitive.

Let's not pretend we didn't know. Let's not pretend we were just victims of circumstance. That doesn't help anybody, especially not us. Because until we take responsibility, we stay stuck in the same cycles.

What Accountability Really Looks Like

Let's define it real simple: Accountability is choosing to take full responsibility for your actions without making excuses.

That means:

- No "I'm sorry if you were hurt."
- No "I didn't mean it like that."
- No "Well, if you hadn't done ___, I wouldn't have done ___."

None of that.

It's: "I did it. I caused the pain. I made that choice. I broke the trust."
And once you own that? You don't just stop there. You work to change. You learn from it. You don't run from the shame, you face it and grow out of it.
Because real maturity doesn't run from hard truths. Real healing isn't about avoiding, it's about addressing.

The Apology That Matters

Let's be honest: a lot of apologies are just words. People say "sorry" all the time. But the kind of apology that heals? That's different.

A real apology sounds like:

- "I understand how I hurt you, and I take full ownership."

Did You Do It? Well, Own It

- "I'm not here to defend what I did. I'm here to take responsibility."
- "I know my actions broke your trust, and I don't expect it back right away. I'm committed to earning it."

And even if the person you hurt doesn't want to hear it… you still have to say it. If only to yourself. If only to God. If only so that you don't stay buried under guilt and shame.

Because unspoken remorse becomes a prison. And the way out is through honesty.

What Happens After You Own It

Now let me warn you, owning your mess doesn't always fix the relationships you broke. Some people may never trust you again. Some damage can't be undone. And that's the reality of life.

But here's what can be fixed…you.

You can become someone who learns from the past. You can grow into a person who doesn't run from the truth. You can be someone who says, "I did it, and I'm not proud of it, but I'm changing."

And let me tell you, there's so much power in that.

When you own your wrongs, you take back your integrity. You stop being a slave to guilt. You look yourself in the mirror and say, "I'm not perfect, but I'm honest. And I'm doing the work."

That's where peace lives. That's where growth lives. That's where trust begins again.

Let Me Talk to the One Who's Struggling With Shame

If this chapter is hitting hard, good. That means your heart's still soft. That means you haven't hardened into the person you were when you broke that trust. That means there's hope for healing.

But let me speak some truth over you: *You are not your mistake.*

You may have caused pain. You may have lied. You may have been selfish. But that's not the end of your story unless you let it be.

You can recover. You can rebuild. You can become better. You just have to be willing to face it.

So say it: "I did it. And I'm ready to grow." "I hurt people. And I'm not going to hide from that." "I can't change what I did. But I can change what I do next."

That's power. That's healing. That's where transformation starts.

Don't Just Own It—Change It

This part's important. You don't just admit the truth and keep living the same way. You commit to a new way of operating.

That means:
- No more gaslighting.
- No more playing victim.
- No more telling half-truths.
- No more pretending like you don't know better.

Did You Do It? Well, Own It

You know better now. So do better now.

Trust is fragile. And once it's broken, it takes time and consistency to rebuild. You can't just apologize once and expect everything to be fixed. You've got to show up. You've got to do the work. You've got to become someone who's worth trusting again.
And trust me, you can. I believe that for you. You just have to decide you're ready.

You're not alone. I've been there too. I've broken trust. I've made bad choices. I've had to face myself and say, "CJ, you did that. And now it's time to fix it."
This chapter wasn't easy to write. And maybe it wasn't easy for you to read. But we can't heal from what we won't own. We can't fix what we won't face.
So let this be the moment you stop pretending. Let this be the chapter where everything changes. Let this be the place where you take your power back. Not by being perfect, but by being honest.
You did it? Then own it. And then go become the version of you who never does it again.

Reflection Questions

1. In what ways have you broken trust with others, and how have you avoided facing it in the past?

2. How does taking full ownership of your actions change the way you see yourself and your healing journey?

3. What does a sincere, responsibility-filled apology look like for you right now? Who (or even what part of yourself) needs to hear it?

4. What new habits or boundaries can you put in place to prevent repeating past mistakes?

5. How can owning your wrongs become a stepping stone toward integrity, freedom, and stronger relationships?

Did You Do It? Well, Own It

Chapter Seventeen

The Peace That Follows Healing

The Peace That Follows Healing

Let's have a moment just you and me again.

You've made it this far in the journey, and that says a lot. You've been willing to dig deep, confront some heavy truths, and peel back the layers of pain, disappointment, and distrust. That's no small thing. That's brave. That's growth. And now, let's talk about the part that doesn't get celebrated enough….the peace that comes on the other side of healing.

Because make no mistake, peace does come.

The Storm Was Necessary—But It's Over Now

Maybe nobody ever told you this, so let me be the first: it wasn't all for nothing. The sleepless nights. The tears. The anxiety. The second-guessing. The wondering if you'd ever trust again, love again, feel safe again.

It wasn't wasted.

See, storms have a way of clearing the air. Of exposing what needs to be rebuilt. Of washing away the things that no longer serve us. Yes, they're chaotic. Yes, they're uncomfortable. But they're also the start of something new.

And when that storm passes—and it will pass—there's a silence that's not empty. It's peaceful. It's sacred. It's healing.

Peace Isn't the Absence of Problems—It's the Presence of Wholeness

Let's get this straight: peace doesn't mean life is perfect. It doesn't mean everyone is treating you right, or that you'll never be disappointed again. What peace really means is this:

You are no longer ruled by the chaos.
You're no longer at war with yourself. You're no longer waiting for the next betrayal. You're no longer walking into every room with suspicion. You're no longer questioning your worth based on how someone else treated you.
Peace is waking up and realizing, "I've healed enough to breathe without fear again."
Peace is finally being okay with what was, because you're grounded in what is.

The Emotional Weight You Didn't Know You Were Carrying

Let's be real. Trust issues are heavy. You carry them everywhere you go. They follow you into relationships, friendships, business deals, even into your spiritual life.

- You second-guess compliments.
- You replay old conversations.
- You anticipate rejection before it ever happens.
- You build exit plans in relationships before they've even begun.

You call it being "cautious," but deep down, you know it's fear wearing a mask.

But when healing comes, so does release. That emotional weight? It starts to fall off.

And suddenly, your shoulders aren't so tense. Your mind isn't running a hundred miles an hour. You're not overanalyzing texts or preparing yourself to be let down.

You're just… present.

That's peace.

What Peace Looks Like in Everyday Life

Let me show you what peace really starts to look like when you've done the work to heal:

- **You trust your gut again**. Not because it's infallible, but because you're finally aligned with your spirit.

- **You stop begging for closure**. You realize some doors don't need to be reopened.

- **You don't fear being alone**. Because you know peace lives inside of you now. Not just in your relationships.

- **You laugh without heaviness**. Because your joy isn't chained to anyone else's approval.

- **You stop performing**. Because your worth isn't on trial anymore.

Peace changes the way you talk, walk, move, and love. It quiets the noise. It sharpens your discernment. It teaches you to trust again, not just people—but yourself, and most importantly, God.

The Peace That Follows Healing

Peace Isn't Weak—It's Powerful

Some people mistake peace for passivity. Like being healed means you're soft or overly forgiving.

Let me tell you something: peace is not weakness.

It takes strength to choose peace after being betrayed. It takes courage to remain open-hearted when the world told you to shut down. It takes discipline to not let bitterness win.

Anyone can be bitter. Anyone can walk away and stay hard. But it takes a healed, mature person to say, "I'm still going to believe the best. I'm still going to show up with love. I'm still going to operate with integrity."

That's strength. That's power. That's what healed peace looks like.

A Word About Internal Peace vs. External Validation

Let's be honest, some of us didn't want healing. We wanted revenge. We didn't want peace. We wanted an apology, or public acknowledgment, or some grand gesture to make it all feel "worth it."

But let me drop this truth on you:

Healing is not dependent upon anyone else doing right by you.

You don't need closure from someone who ghosted you. You don't need validation from someone who manipulated you. You don't need a co-sign from someone who never saw your value.

Peace doesn't come when they change. It comes when you do.

So stop waiting for people to act right before you let go of the pain. That's giving them too much power. Choose peace anyway. Heal anyway. Move forward anyway.

What Healing Peace Sounds Like

Let me tell you some of the things that start to come out of your mouth when peace starts replacing pain:
- "That hurt me, but it doesn't own me anymore."
- "I'm grateful for what it taught me, even if it broke me at the time."
- "I wish them well, even though they did me wrong."
- "I don't need revenge. I've got peace."
- "I still believe in love."

Now tell me that's not freedom.

Tell me that's not God at work. Tell me that's not the other side of the mountain you've been climbing.

Don't Let Peace Scare You

This one might sound odd, but I have to say it…some people are so used to chaos that peace feels unsafe.

They've lived in dysfunction so long that when things finally get quiet, they panic. "This is too good to be true." "Something bad is about to happen." "I can't trust this peace."

If that's you, breathe. Sit in the stillness. Stop waiting for the other shoe to drop.

Peace doesn't mean something bad is coming. It means something good is already here.

You deserve this.
You've fought for this.
Let yourself have it.

What God's Peace Really Feels Like

Now we gotta talk about this.

There's no peace like the peace that comes from God. The Bible says it's the kind of peace that passes all understanding, which means it doesn't always make sense to people around you. It doesn't always match your circumstances. But it's real. It's deep. It's solid.

You'll be in the middle of transition and still have rest. You'll be facing uncertainty and still feel stable. You'll be healing from betrayal and still feel surrounded by grace.

That's not just emotional peace. That's spiritual alignment. That's what happens when you start trusting God again, not just with your eternity, but with your today.

Let's Reflect: Are You Allowing Peace In?

Let me ask you this—and answer honestly:

- Are you still replaying the betrayal in your mind every day?
- Are you holding on to hurt because it gives you a reason not to trust?
- Are you afraid of what life looks like without your walls?
- Have you become so familiar with brokenness that you don't know how to live in healing?

If any of that hits… it's time to let peace in.

Trust Issues

It's time to believe that your story doesn't have to end in pain. It's time to accept that you don't need drama to feel alive. It's time to declare: "I'm ready for peace. And I won't sabotage it when it comes."

After all the battles you've fought…internally and externally…after the pain, the grief, the forgiveness, the work…

You've earned this peace.

You've earned the right to sleep without anxiety. You've earned the right to love without fear. You've earned the right to breathe again.

Don't downplay that. Don't run from that. Don't question if you're worthy of it.

You are.

You're not who you were. You're healing. You're evolving. You're whole. And this peace? This is your reward for not giving up when it would've been easier to stay bitter.

So take a deep breath. Close your eyes. Feel the stillness.

This is what healing looks like.

This is what peace feels like.

This is the beginning of everything new.

Reflection Questions

1. What old emotional weights are you still carrying, and how can you begin to release them?

2. How does peace show up in your daily life now compared to before you started healing?

3. What's the difference between seeking external validation and experiencing God's inner peace for yourself?

4. When was the last time you felt true stillness with God, and what did it teach you?

5. How can you remind yourself that you are worthy of peace, even when life isn't perfect?

Trust Issues

Chapter Eighteen

Stronger Relationships After Healing

Stronger Relationships After Healing

Can I just say something right out the gate?

You deserve love that doesn't make you flinch. You deserve connection that feels safe. You deserve to be trusted and to trust again.

But here's the truth: those kinds of relationships don't just show up, they grow after you've done the healing.

Because healing reshapes your heart. Healing resets your standards. Healing reintroduces you to yourself.

And when you've done that work? That inner, gritty, truth-telling, mirror-facing work? That's when everything changes. That's when your relationships stop looking like survival and start looking like peace.

What Healing Does to Your Relationships

Let's break this down.

When you're still wounded, your relationships reflect your wounds. You move from fear. You communicate through insecurity. You build walls instead of bridges. You test people instead of trusting them. And sometimes, you sabotage the very thing you prayed for because you're still living in yesterday's pain.

But healing changes the entire game.

Stronger Relationships After Healing

- You stop needing to be in control all the time.
- You stop interpreting silence as rejection.
- You stop turning little misunderstandings into big explosions.
- You stop needing constant reassurance to feel safe.

Healing makes space for real intimacy. For honest conversations. For quiet moments that don't feel awkward. For love that feels like partnership, not punishment.

You Choose Better When You're Healed

One of the biggest blessings of healing is clarity.

When your vision is no longer clouded by fear, abandonment, and betrayal, you start seeing people for who they really are…not who you want them to be or who you're afraid they are.

You stop settling. You stop choosing out of desperation. You stop attaching to brokenness that mirrors your past.

Healing helps you recognize:

- "This feels familiar, but it's not healthy."
- "This looks good, but it's not good for me."
- "This relationship is peaceful, and I don't need to sabotage it just because it's new."

You begin to choose love that's grounded. Friendships that uplift. Partnerships that feel like home.

Trust Becomes a Bridge, Not a Barrier

When trust issues run deep, you build barriers to protect yourself. And that made sense then. But now? You're healed. Or at least, healing. And trust isn't supposed to keep people out, it's supposed to help the right people come in.

Healing helps you:

- Set healthy boundaries without building emotional prisons.
- Give people a chance without setting traps to prove they'll fail.
- Trust yourself to walk away when things no longer serve you.

You're not naïve anymore. You're not bitter either. You're wise. You're discerning. And you know that trust is a bridge to connection, not a wall to loneliness.

You Attract What You Are

Let me say this with love:

If you keep attracting chaos, inconsistency, or toxicity... it might be time to look inward.

But the beautiful part is—once you've done the work, once you've healed those broken parts, once you've reclaimed your value—you'll notice a shift. You start attracting people who:

- Match your energy.
- Honor your boundaries.

Stronger Relationships After Healing

- Respect your journey.
- Speak your language of love.

Healing puts out a different signal. You stop vibrating at the level of your trauma and start vibrating at the level of your truth. And that energy? It draws in healthier, stronger, more meaningful connections.

Conflict Doesn't Scare You Anymore

Before healing, conflict felt like the end. One disagreement, and you'd spiral. You'd either shut down or blow up. You'd start preparing your exit or bracing for betrayal.

But now?

Now you realize conflict is normal. And healthy relationships aren't about avoiding it, they're about navigating it with grace.

- You don't weaponize silence.
- You don't run at the first sign of tension.
- You don't let your trauma speak louder than your truth.

You communicate. You listen. You compromise.
That's growth. That's healing in action.

You Create a Safe Space—for You and Others

One of the best parts of healing? You become a safe space.

- Safe for honesty.
- Safe for vulnerability.
- Safe for accountability.

- Safe for love.

You no longer bring chaos into every room you enter. You no longer leave people guessing how you feel. You no longer bleed on people who didn't cut you.

And because you've become a safe space, you attract people who are safe too. Who can handle your truth. Who don't use your past against you. Who see you as whole, not broken.

You Deserve This

You've come a long way. And now? You're ready for relationships that reflect your growth.

You deserve friendships that don't require performance. You deserve love that doesn't cost you your peace. You deserve connection that's built on truth, not trauma.

Don't let your past rob you of the good things God has waiting for you. You're not who you used to be. So don't settle for relationships that belong to the old you.

Step boldly into this next chapter. Show up with your healed self. And don't be afraid to receive love that feels unfamiliar.

Because the healed version of you? They know how to handle it. They're ready for it. They were built for this.

Reflection Questions

1. How have your relationships in the past reflected your unhealed wounds?

2. What new relational standards have you set for yourself now that you're on a healing journey?

3. How do you know the difference between building healthy boundaries and building emotional walls?

4. In what ways has healing made you a safer space for yourself and others?

5. What type of relationships do you now believe you truly deserve, and how will you position yourself to receive them?

Chapter Nineteen

Emotional Freedom — The Blessing of Releasing the Burden

Emotional Freedom — The Blessing of Releasing the Burden

Let me tell you something real: there is no heavier baggage than the weight of broken trust. It clings to your thoughts, slips into your conversations, hijacks your relationships, and camps out in your spirit. You don't even realize it, but you've been carrying it for years. And the longer it stays, the more damage it does. But here's the good news—on the other side of healing, there's a blessing that doesn't get talked about enough: emotional freedom.

Yes. Freedom. Peace in your chest. Lightness in your soul. A mind that's not constantly replaying scenarios or rehearsing pain. That kind of freedom is real. And it's waiting on the other side of the decision to heal.

What Emotional Bondage Looks Like

Before we celebrate freedom, let's talk about what it feels like to be emotionally bound. Because if you've ever been in that place, you know it's not just sad—it's suffocating.

- You second-guess every person in your life.

- You overthink texts, silence, compliments, and even kindness.
- You assume people are out to hurt you.
- You keep your heart locked behind walls that no one gets through...not even you.
- You carry resentment like a shield.

And worse, you think it's normal. You start believing this is just the way life is. That you're "protecting" yourself. That if you let go of the anger or fear, you'll get hurt all over again.

But that's not protection. That's prison.

Freedom Is a Heart Set Free

Emotional freedom doesn't mean forgetting what happened. It doesn't mean pretending it didn't hurt. It means you're no longer driven by that hurt. It doesn't get to dictate how you show up anymore.

When you're emotionally free:

- You can trust without needing guarantees.
- You can love without expecting betrayal.
- You can give grace without fearing it will be taken advantage of.
- You can speak truth without bitterness.
- You can receive love without suspicion.

It's not about becoming careless, it's about becoming clear. Clear in your boundaries, your emotions, your healing, and your intentions.

What Stands in the Way of Emotional Freedom

Let's be honest. Some of us aren't free because we refuse to release. We're still rehearsing what they did, reliving the betrayal, replaying the pain like a broken record.

Why? Because we're afraid. Afraid that letting go means they "win." That moving on means it didn't matter. That if we heal, we'll forget how bad it really was.

But that's not true.

You don't heal for them. You heal for you. You release not because what they did was okay, but because you refuse to stay bound by it any longer.

Freedom costs something, yes—but staying in chains costs even more.

The Day You Decide to Let Go

There comes a moment in healing when you realize something simple but powerful: you don't want to carry this anymore. That moment is everything.

You stop rehearsing the clapbacks you never said. You stop stalking their socials. You stop looking for evidence that validates your pain. You stop needing apologies you might never get.

And you say to yourself, "I choose peace. I choose joy. I choose freedom."

That's the day everything starts changing.

Emotional Freedom — The Blessing of Releasing the Burden

How Freedom Feels (And What It Looks Like)

Freedom doesn't just feel good, it looks good on you. You glow different. You move different. People can feel when you're not carrying bitterness. They can tell when your joy is real. They're drawn to it.

Some signs you're walking in emotional freedom:

- You're not easily triggered by your past.
- You can talk about what happened without breaking down or lashing out.
- You're no longer trying to prove your worth.
- You forgive quicker—not because you're weak, but because you're wise.
- You celebrate others—even those who hurt you—because your peace isn't petty.

It's emotional maturity. It's spiritual growth. It's healing in full effect.

Letting God Heal What You've Hidden

Some of the deepest emotional wounds are the ones we've hidden the longest. We told ourselves we were "fine." We moved on... kind of. But deep down, we buried the betrayal, the rejection, the abandonment.
God wants access to that.
He's not asking you to heal yourself. He's asking you to invite Him in.
Let God into the places you've sealed off. Let Him touch what you've guarded for years. Let Him free you from what you thought was protecting you.

Trust Issues

Because when God heals a wound, He doesn't just cover it—He transforms it. And the scar becomes a testimony, not a trigger.

You were not created to live weighed down by what happened. Trust issues, betrayal, fear—none of it has the final say. Freedom is not just a concept. It's a real life you can live, starting now.

So take a breath. Choose release. Choose healing. Choose freedom.

Your future deserves it.

Reflection Questions

1. What emotions are you still carrying that keep you from living freely?

2. Who do you need to forgive—not for them, but for your freedom?

3. What has emotional bondage cost you?

4. What does emotional freedom look like for you personally?

Chapter Twenty

The Reward of Wholeness

The Reward of Wholeness

You've made it. This chapter may be the last, but don't be fooled—it's not the end. It's the beginning of a whole new you. You've journeyed through the depths of pain, the confusion of broken trust, and the challenges of healing. You've faced yourself in ways that weren't easy, but you did it. And now, as you stand on the other side of it, there's one undeniable truth: you are whole again.

This is the reward of healing from trust issues, the gift of becoming whole. And let me tell you, this doesn't just mean getting past your wounds. It means building yourself back up—stronger, wiser, and more resilient than you ever thought possible.

The Transformation From Brokenness to Wholeness

Healing doesn't erase the past. You still remember the hurt, the betrayals, the pain. But it doesn't hold power over you anymore. You've been transformed.

You see, when you begin to heal, your perception shifts. You begin to see yourself as someone worthy of trust, someone capable of trusting again. You stop identifying as "broken" or "damaged" and start realizing that you're a masterpiece in

The Reward of Wholeness

progress. You are not the sum of your past failures or the people who hurt you. You are the sum of your resilience, your growth, your strength, and your willingness to love again—despite it all.

Here's what wholeness looks like in action:

- **Confidence in your decisions**: You no longer second-guess your choices. Trusting yourself becomes second nature. You know when to say yes and when to walk away.

- **Freedom in your heart**: You carry less emotional baggage. The heaviness of past hurts no longer weighs you down. Your heart is lighter, and your spirit is unburdened.

- **Healthy relationships**: Your ability to trust others has been restored, but this time it's different. You set boundaries, you speak your truth, and you trust without fear of betrayal. You've learned that trusting others doesn't mean you're giving away your power, it means you're inviting people in who are worthy of your trust.

- **A renewed sense of purpose**: As you've healed, you've found your voice. You've learned who you are and what you stand for. You're more aligned with your values and more focused on your path. Your purpose isn't clouded by distrust or fear anymore; it's crystal clear.

- **Inner peace**: There's a calmness inside you that wasn't there before. The storm inside your soul has settled. You can rest in peace because you know that no matter what comes your way, you've got the strength to handle it. You don't need to control every situation, you just need to trust in the process.

The Strength of Vulnerability

One of the most beautiful byproducts of healing is the power of vulnerability. When we're broken, we hide. We protect our hearts with walls that no one can get through. But in the process of healing, those walls begin to crumble. And what replaces them? Strength. True strength.

When you're whole, you can be vulnerable without fearing rejection or betrayal. You can open your heart to others without expecting them to disappoint you. Your vulnerability becomes your superpower, because it's not about being weak or fragile—it's about being authentic. You can show up as your true self without needing to hide behind the armor of distrust.

And here's the thing: when you allow yourself to be vulnerable, others begin to trust you more. They see the authenticity, the openness, the realness—and they're drawn to it. You set the example of what it looks like to heal and move forward. You lead with your heart open, and that's what attracts real, meaningful connections into your life.

The Beauty of Forgiveness

Wholeness is closely linked to forgiveness. But forgiveness doesn't mean excusing the wrongs done to you. It doesn't mean you forget what happened or let people off the hook. It means you release the power those wrongs have over you. It means you stop allowing the bitterness, resentment, and anger to control your emotions. You forgive, not because they deserve it, but because you deserve peace.

When you've healed, you can forgive freely. You can release others from the hold of your pain. And when you do, you free yourself too. It's not about them, it's about you finding your peace. You stop giving them control over your emotional well-being, and instead, you choose to live in the freedom of forgiveness.

Forgiveness doesn't make the hurt go away, but it allows you to move forward without the chains of bitterness. And as you forgive others, you also learn to forgive yourself. You stop punishing yourself for past mistakes and begin to accept that healing is a process. You're not perfect, and that's okay.

The Role of Trust in a Whole Life

Wholeness and trust are inseparable. Without trust, there's no real connection. Without trust, there's no true intimacy in relationships. But here's the difference now: your trust has been rebuilt. You trust yourself, you trust others, and most importantly, you trust God. You've learned that trust isn't about expecting perfection from people, it's about expecting honesty, integrity, and respect.

You don't need to control every situation or every relationship. You've learned that trust doesn't mean being blind to the flaws of others—it means recognizing their humanity and accepting that while they may hurt you, they also have the capacity to love you, support you, and walk alongside you.

Your new level of trust is grounded in wisdom. You've learned how to give trust without giving away your power. You've learned how to trust others while still maintaining healthy boundaries and a sense of self.

Living in the Blessing of Wholeness

What happens when you live in this place of wholeness? You stop running from life. You stop playing small. You stop letting the mistakes of your past determine your future. Instead, you stand strong, confident in who you are, and trust that the people, opportunities, and experiences you need will come into your life at the right time.

The reward of wholeness is the ability to live fully and freely. You're no longer afraid of being hurt or disappointed. You trust that no matter what life throws at you, you have the strength to handle it. You know that even when things don't go as planned, you're still okay. You are whole, and nothing outside of you can take that away.

Wholeness brings a peace that surpasses understanding. It's a peace that doesn't depend on external circumstances. It's a peace that's rooted in the trust you've built, the healing you've received, and the confidence you now carry in your spirit.

Final Word:

You've done the work. You've walked through the pain. You've faced your fears. And now, you're standing on the other side. **Whole. Free. Empowered.**

This is the reward of healing. It's not just about overcoming trust issues it's about becoming the person you were always meant to be. And now, you can live fully, love freely, and trust deeply, knowing that you are whole, and no one and nothing can take that away from you.

The Reward of Wholeness

Reflection Questions

1. How does it feel to think of yourself as whole, rather than broken?

2. In what ways has trust played a role in your healing process?

3. What do you think you need to continue healing and growing as a whole person?

4. How will you protect you're wholeness going forward?

Trust Issues

The Reward of Wholeness

Welcome to the life you deserve!

Acknowledgments

Writing Trust Issues has been one of the most personal journeys of my life. This book is not just a project it's a piece of my heart, my healing, my testimony. And I couldn't have made it here without so many people who walked alongside me. Some cheering, some challenging, but all contributing to the man I am today.

And to those who hurt me, doubted me, and challenged me…thank you, too. Your actions, though painful, pushed me closer to God, closer to healing, and closer to the man I was always meant to become. Without the storms, I wouldn't have learned to trust God the way I do now. You played a part in this story, too.

This book is for anyone who's ever struggled to trust again. For anyone who's ever been broken and dared to believe healing was still possible. Thank you all for being part of my story to God be the glory always.

- Cj Morgan

Notes

1. *See Psalms 77:11-12 NIV - pg. 99*
2. *See Proverbs 3:5-6 NIV - pg. 100, 115*
3. *See Joshua 1:9 NIV - pg. 100*
4. *See Philippians 4:6-7 NIV - pg. 101*
5. *See Luke 22:42 NIV - pg 101*
6. *See Psalm 9:10 NIV - pg 102*
7. *See Isaiah 40:31 NIV - pg 103*
8. *See Proverbs 27:17 NIV - pg 104*
9. *See Psalms 34:18 NIV - pg 107*
10. *See Ephesians 4:22-24 NIV - pg 108*
11. *See Isaiah 43:1 NIV - pg. 109*
12. *See Philippians 1:6 NIV - pg. 110*
13. *See Isaiah 43:18-19 NIV - pg. 111*
14. *See Romans 8:28 NIV - pg. 112, 116*
15. *See James 1:2-4 NIV - pg. 117*
16. *See Psalms 23:4 NIV - pg. 118*
17. *See Matthew 6:34 NIV - pg. 119*
18. *See Proverbs 16:9 NIV - pg. 119*

About The Author

C.J. Morgan is a visionary, devoted husband, proud father of six, and passionate minister on a mission to empower and inspire. Born and raised in the vibrant city of Houston, Texas, C.J.'s journey in ministry began in 2005 when he received a profound calling to serve. His spiritual foundation was further strengthened by the unwavering support and guidance of his parents, Apostle C.D. Morgan Sr. and Pastor Dinah Morgan.

As a man of faith, family, and community, C.J. balances his roles with grace and purpose. His marriage to Jalika Cherie Morgan is a testament to love, partnership, and shared commitment to their family and calling. Together, they are raising their six children in an environment of faith, love, and the pursuit of excellence.

C.J.'s ministry is marked by his diverse spiritual gifts and his genuine passion for uplifting others. His vision extends far beyond the pulpit; he is dedicated to cultivating future leaders who are rooted in strong values and equipped to make a positive impact. Through mentorship, teaching, and by personal example, he encourages individuals to build meaningful relationships, fostering a sense of community and mutual support.

A firm believer in the power of knowledge, C.J. is an advocate for continuous learning and personal growth. He inspires those around him to never cease in their pursuit of wisdom, understanding that education - both spiritual and secular - is a lifelong journey that empowers individuals to reach their full potential.

In every aspect of his life - as a minister, husband, father, mentor, and community leader - C.J. Morgan embodies the principles of faith, love, and purpose. His life's work is a testament to the transformative power of living with intentionality and serving others with a heart full of compassion and a mind open to endless possibilities.

Made in the USA
Monee, IL
15 September 2025

24765343R00125